ORIENTAL WISDOM

Tathagat Anand Srivastava lives in Dehradun and is a student of Class XII in St. Joseph's Academy. He started writing at the tender age of seven and had his first book published in 2019, when he was only ten. *Oriental Wisdom* is his third book.

He loves reading a wide range of books, both fiction and non-fiction, and this diversity is reflected in his writing. His other interests include singing, playing the guitar, watching movies, and public speaking.

You can reach him on:
Instagram: https://instagram.com/tathagat.anand007
Facebook: https://www.facebook.com/people/Tathagat-Anand/100064180505761/

ORIENTAL WISDOM

Odysseys of a Young Indian

Tathagat Anand Srivastava

RUPA

Published by
Rupa Publications India Pvt. Ltd 2025
161-B/4, Gulmohar House,
Yusuf Sarai Community Centre,
New Delhi 110049

Sales centres
Bengaluru Chennai
Hyderabad Kolkata Mumbai

P-ISBN: 978-93-7003-614-7
E-ISBN: 978-93-7003-391-7

First impression 2025

10 9 8 7 6 5 4 3 2 1

Printed in India

I humbly dedicate this book
to my loving grandmother,
Mrs Dayawati Srivastava,
who never fails to inspire me with her 'never-say-die' attitude,
and continually enriches my thoughts and life
with her vast wisdom—oriental or otherwise.

Contents

The Planning: Dehradun / 1

Day 1: New Delhi to Singapore / 9

Day 2: Singapore / 17

Day 3: Singapore / 26

Day 4: Singapore / 35

Day 5: Singapore to Kuala Lumpur / 53

Day 6: Kuala Lumpur / 63

Day 7: Kuala Lumpur / 73

Day 8: Kuala Lumpur to Bangkok and Pattaya / 82

Day 9: Pattaya / 91

Day 10: Pattaya to Bangkok / 101

Day 11: Bangkok / 111

Day 12: Bangkok to Bali / 120

Day 13: Bali / 131

Day 14: Bali / 142

Day 15: Bali to Delhi / 151

Oriental Wisdom / 160

Acknowledgements / 165

oriental wisdom. the accumulated wisdom of Eastern cultures, including philosophies, religions, and practices; offering perspectives on life, the universe, and human existence.

Experiences count. More so, when you gain them through travelling. Good experiences turn into good memories, which you cherish for years. Bad experiences are not that bad though. They turn into wonderful stories.

The Planning: Dehradun

'Why can't we go to Kerala during the vacations? Don't you think it's the most beautiful state in India? Serene backwaters, marvellous beaches, and wonderful people.'

'Yes, dear, Kerala is beautiful. I love going there. The only problem is that we've already visited four times and seen every corner of the state.'

'Sir, you did enjoy every time, no?'

'Yes, ma'am, we all did. No doubt about that.'

'All the more reason to go there once again. Instead of going to a new place without being sure whether we'll enjoy it or not, Kerala seems to be a far better option.'

'Well, we could try visiting some other places too. What if they turn out to be as good as Kerala, and the saree stores are equally good?'

'Why do you always have to blame it on sarees, huh? There are numerous things to see when you're visiting a place.'

'Yes, of course. Like the jewellery shops.'

'Oh yes, that reminds me of Tamil Nadu. Last time we were there, I missed out on some new varieties of conch shell jewellery. Moreover, the greenery is unparalleled and the temples are beautiful. We could plan another trip to the state.'

'A new place, maybe?'

'Like? See, there's no point going to Europe in winter. Same goes for the hilly states in India.'

'Andaman and Nicobar Islands could be a good option.'

'I'll have to do some research before I say yes.'

Mumma and Dad were planning the upcoming winter trip. Generally, when they discuss our holiday plans, I sit back and enjoy the show. Dad, as usual, started with a SWOT analysis, while Mumma countered with the latest fashion trends and shopping hotspots. Their discussions are like a masterclass in negotiation and a sitcom rolled into one, with this one being no exception.

My school was scheduled to be closed for 25 days after my half-yearly exams were over. A long winter trip was on the cards—and in our family, it was normal to start discussing the plan months in advance.

Dad is like a Swiss watch: punctual, precise, and a bit too obsessed with schedules. He's a go-getter, a walking management school in sensible shoes. Mumma, on the other hand, is a charmer with a black belt in the art of persuasion and a knack for making friends with store clerks. Together, they're the perfect blend of efficiency and style. As for me, I aspire to learn these traits, as long as they don't involve early morning showers or marathon shopping sessions.

We all had different ideas about a winter trip. As a junior school student, these trips were a welcome break from the mundane routine of school, homework, and a nervous friend's incessant need to borrow my notes.

Mumma, ever the connoisseur, is always more interested in enjoying the natural and artistic beauty of places, taking innumerable selfies, and buying the best of local sarees, jewellery, spices, souvenirs, and whatnot. Dad has a unique opinion about travelling. He believes that true education comes from exposing oneself to the world. So, a trip is an opportunity for him to meet different people, learn about their cultures, and even speak their languages. Maybe because of this, he's very fond of watching travel channels, and his library is full of Lonely Planet guides and language-learning books.

I was absolutely loving the endless discussion between my parents when a voice, somewhat sounding like my name, interrupted my entertainment. It was Dad suggesting to Mumma that I should also have a say in the final decision.

'Shouldn't we ask Joy?'

'Yes, of course. He enjoys it every time we go to South India.'

'Maybe he'll like seeing a new place.'

'Why not?'

So, finally, at the age of 12, I now qualified as someone whose opinion counted. Wow!

'Joy, what do you say?'

'Dad, why don't we go somewhere outside India? I haven't seen much of the world yet.'

'Really? You've already been to a number of countries with us.'

'Dad, practically speaking, it'll be my first trip abroad.'

'And the trips to the UK and the US don't mean anything?'

'Dad! I was literally in your lap when we visited the US. I hardly remember anything from that trip. Yes, I do have some faint memories of our UK trip, but when I see the photographs, it feels like I've forgotten most of it.'

'Yes, I see the point. So, where would you like to go?'

'We could go to Disneyland.'

'That's all?'

'And wherever you want to go after that.'

'Joy, we should go to a place that's naturally beautiful and has entertainment options too.'

'I tell you what. We could go to the UAE. Joy will definitely enjoy Ferrari World in Abu Dhabi, and Sharjah is a culturally rich city,' Mumma chipped in.

'Yes, it's a good option. Additionally, Dubai is a shopping paradise,' Dad said in a very sincere manner. But, somehow, in my mind, I sensed a subtle sarcasm in his voice. He was deliberately pointing out the 'shopping' bit.

Mumma too sensed the sarcasm, but laughed it off, saying, 'Yeah, we can stay in Dubai and plan day trips to nearby islands.'

'Yes! Let's finalize it. We'll go to the UAE.' I felt excited about the prospect of visiting Ferrari World.

'Joy, UAE is a good option. But the trip will be a short one, as there's no point staying in Dubai for more than a week. We've about 15 to 20 days with us. We could plan another country after that.'

'From there, we can go to Kenya. You've always wanted to go there, haven't you?' Mumma said to Dad.

'I want to go to Kenya for a different reason. I want to travel the length of the country at my own pace—backpacking, sort of, you know. So, six to seven days may not be enough. I'd need something closer to a month to do that,' Dad said, closing his eyes as if imagining his dream backpacking excursion.

'Any other place in Africa?'

'In my opinion, there's a lot to see and learn in Africa. We'll plan an extended journey to the continent. We shouldn't mix it with other places.'

'Yes, of course.' Mumma and I nodded in agreement. Not because we had the same opinion as Dad, but more out of apprehension that if we didn't, the 'Real Education' lecture would follow and continue till eternity.

Now, we had to choose a destination that offered something for all of us. It needed to be rich in culture, history, and tradition, providing a new learning experience. It also had to have places like amusement parks, so that I could have a good time. And, it goes without saying, it had to be a shopper's paradise. I had to make the most of Geography and General Knowledge expertise I had acquired by the seventh standard. I requested a time-out, which was granted without any hassles, as Dad and Mumma continued exploring the possibilities of surviving in different parts of the globe.

When I rejoined them after an hour, they were still debating between Australia and South America. I felt happy that my suggestion to go abroad was being taken seriously, and no Indian state featured in their discussion anymore. Dad was all for South America, while Mumma was now leaning towards Australia.

'Australia is very, very big, dear. It would take a lifetime if we planned to travel along the coastline alone,' Dad presented his logic against Australia.

'We could skip the main cities and focus on the outback.'

'Is there anything beyond the main cities? You'd be skipping practically the whole country. If you ask me, we should start with Argentina, and then go to Peru in the second half. I've always wanted to see Machu Picchu. Besides, we're all learning Spanish, and it'll give us a good chance to brush up our skills.'

'Yes, I understand. We must to go to South America, just because you guys are learning Spanish with the help of a funny mobile app.' Mumma was definitely not happy about the proposition.

'See, the app is not meant to be funny—it's genuinely effective. *Podemos hablar español ahora, todos de nosotros.*'

So, now the direction of the discussion shifted from the place of vacation to the efficiency of this Spanish app we all were using. Dad was all in favour of it, and proved his point by speaking a complete sentence in Spanish. Bravo! Here I knew, it was time for me to enter the conversation.

'Dad, Mumma, we should go to East Asia—three or four countries. These countries are rich in culture and will help us gain real education. We'll have a lot of fun activities, and all of them are good shopping destinations.' Thankfully, both my parents failed to sense the sarcasm that I intentionally inserted by using the terms 'real education' and 'shopping'. They seemed genuinely interested.

'Go on,' said Dad.

'Dad, my suggestion is to visit Singapore, Thailand, and Indonesia. I want to see the Universal Studios in Singapore. We could enjoy a cruise evening in Bangkok, and finally celebrate the New Year in Bali. What do you say?'

'Not a bad idea. We can do Malaysia too. Kuala Lumpur is not far from Singapore, and I'll have a chance to meet an old friend there.'

'Kuala Lumpur is not far from Singapore?'

'Not that far.'

'Like, how many kilometres?'

'Around 350,' he quickly and almost proudly replied, without having to consult any source. I could see his eyes beaming with the expression, 'This is my field of expertise, you idiot!' Thanks, Lonely Planet.

'That doesn't seem too far. We could try going on a road trip to Kuala Lumpur, as it will allow us to experience the "scenic beauty" of surrounding areas,' I said, inserting another bit of sarcasm with the phrase 'scenic beauty.'

'Good idea! We'll definitely do it. Now, you guys give me the list of places you want to see, and I will prepare a day-wise itinerary.'

'If we are going to Bangkok, we can add the floating market to the list. It will be a great experience,' Mumma said.

'For sure. Let's prepare the list then.'

A week later, we were ready with an action plan. Dad had prepared an elaborate itinerary. I was quite sure, given his fascination with minute details, he had possibly included even the meal timings and the names of Indian restaurants where we were going to have lunch. And who knows—even the names of the waiters who would be serving us in those restaurants!

According to the minute-to-minute program, we were going to Delhi first, then flying to Singapore. From there, we would take a road trip to Kuala Lumpur in Malaysia, continue on to Bangkok and Pattaya in Thailand, and finally head to Bali, Indonesia. The program included a list of all the places we were going to visit, complete with exact timings. It goes without saying that the list was impressive—it included all sorts of activities: monuments, zoological gardens, shopping places, water sports, and even two cruise safaris. Wow! This was going to be a memorable trip.

By the time my exams were over, Dad had everything ready with the help of a tour operator. Visas, air tickets, hotel bookings, internal transfers, vouchers for different activities, tickets for monuments—and what not. The only deviation from the original plan was that the tour operator didn't book a direct flight to Singapore from Delhi, owing to some cost considerations. Instead, we were booked on a connecting flight to Singapore via Kuala Lumpur. The layover time at Kuala Lumpur (KL) airport was nearly 4 hours, and we were supposed to reach Singapore the next morning. Alright—if it saves some bucks.

Day 1

New Delhi to Singapore

Our flight to Kuala Lumpur was at 9.30 p.m. from Indira Gandhi International Airport, New Delhi. It was clearly mentioned in Dad's minute-to-minute program that we would start from Dehradun in the morning, take some rest at a hotel in Aerocity, and reach the airport by 7 p.m.

Sticking to the plan, we started our journey from Dehradun in a taxi around 8 in the morning, and reached Aerocity around 1 in the afternoon. As everything was already taken care of, we had a smooth check-in at our chosen hotel. After resting for a while in the hotel room, we came down to the lounge, which was full of smiling faces. People were busy talking to one another.

We got seated, and Mumma went to bring some coffee. I started to look around the lounge. It was big and beautiful. While looking around, my eyes settled on a group of three people in a corner. By their expressions and behaviour, it was not difficult to deduce that they were a family—a man, a woman, and a 13–14-year-old boy. The woman was trying to show something on her mobile to the man, while the man didn't seem interested. He was looking at his own mobile with a worried face. The boy, on the other hand, was calmly looking around, just like me. We made eye contact and he smiled. I smiled back and waved to him.

I guess he was waiting for this, because before I could end smiling, he came to me and said hi.

'Hi,' I said warmly.

'I'm Aryan. We are from Indore.'

'My name is Joy. We live in Dehradun.'

'You're going somewhere or coming back?'

'We are going to Singapore.'

'I'd have guessed,' he smiled. His smile was very friendly, and I immediately liked him.

'How could you? What if we're here to visit Delhi only?'

'Oh, then you wouldn't stay here in Aerocity.'

'You have a point,' I smiled again.

'So, is it going to be only Singapore, or will you be going any further?'

'We've a long trip ahead. We'll take a flight to Kuala Lumpur tonight. Tomorrow at 7 in the morning, we've got a flight from KL to Singapore. We'll spend three to four days in Singapore. From there, we'll go to Malaysia for three days, then Thailand, and finally Indonesia. What about you guys? Where are you going?'

'We are going back to Indore,' he laughed.

'And where are you coming back from?'

'As of now, from Kuala Lumpur. We went to Vietnam first and then to Malaysia.'

'How was it? Did you enjoy it there?' I couldn't control my curiosity.

'Well, that depends on how you define enjoyment,' Aryan was being philosophical. The way he closed his eyes and smiled after saying this made me more curious. What exactly did that mean?

'Hmm, did you see many tourist attractions?'

'Yes, we did. But more importantly, I enjoyed the smaller things.'

'Like?'

'You'll know yourself. Is this your first trip abroad?'

'Not exactly. Dad and Mom took me to USA when I was an infant—no memories at all. Then, I was still in kindergarten when I was taken to England and Scotland. Don't remember much of it as well. So, I'm not in a position to say whether I enjoyed them or not.'

'Do you think you'll enjoy this trip?'

'I suppose so.'

'Then you will. See, a trip is not just about visiting the tourist attractions. I mean, they are important, but meeting the locals, exchanging ideas with them and learning from their way of living teaches you a lot.'

'You're speaking like a grown-up. How old are you, Aryan bhai?'

'I am fourteen. And I guess, it's a pretty ripe age to understand what makes you feel happy and satisfied. How old are you?'

'I'm twelve. Still waiting to attain a ripe age.'

'Ha ha. See, if your concepts about life are clear, then age doesn't bar you from seeing things from a right perspective. And travelling is one thing that makes you learn enormously. You'll feel that yourself after coming back from this trip.'

'Aryan bhai, we've a very tightly packed schedule for the trip, and that is going to keep us busier than a one-armed paper hanger. I wonder if I'll get any chance to see and talk to the locals. Moreover, my parents think I'm still very young, and they might not approve of me talking to strangers.'

'Keep your eyes and ears open during the trip. You will

get plenty of opportunities to speak to people and learn from your surroundings. I'm sure, you'll come back a wiser man.'

'Let's see. Now tell me one thing—why is your Dad looking worried? Is everything okay?'

'Oh, it's nothing. Papa is a workaholic. Although he's on leave, his mind is on office matters. He has a constant feeling that his subordinates won't work in his absence, so he's taking a report from each one of them. In fact, he didn't want to come on this trip in the first place. Mummy and I had to do a hell of a lot of work to convince him somehow. Let me introduce you to them.'

I greeted Aryan's father, who smiled at me, greeted back, and returned to his official business. Aryan was right about his papa. Papaji's raised eyebrows had nothing to do with Aryan or his mother—he was simply too absorbed in his work.

Aryan grinned and shrugged. 'Papa ji is like this only,' he said.

Dad and Mumma finished their coffee, I said goodbye to Aryan, and we went back to our room.

Our flight to Kuala Lumpur was supposed to leave at 9.30 p.m., so we had quite a bit of time on our hands. The three of us began sharing our respective ideas for how to spend it. Among these suggestions, two were shortlisted and labelled as 'rational courses of action' by our adorable timekeeper—dear Dad.

'Since our flight is at 9.30 p.m., we've to reach the airport by 7 p.m. under any circumstances. So, we can either stay here at the hotel and rest, or we can check out and watch a movie or something,' Dad said.

Since no one was in the mood to sleep just yet, we chose the latter course. Mumma started looking at a couple of different shows nearby, and soon booked the tickets for *Jumanji: The*

Next Level. The show was scheduled to start at 3.30 p.m. at the movie theatre in Ambience Mall, which was about 6 minutes from our hotel, according to Google Maps. Fair enough.

We checked out of the hotel, loaded our taxi with the luggage, and set off. The mall was indeed very close to Aerocity, and it didn't take us more than seven minutes to reach it. At 3.30 p.m. sharp, we got seated in the movie hall, but the movie hadn't started yet, and all we could see was an advertisement highlighting the efficacy of a certain face wash, followed by an advertisement of a 'beautifying face cream' from the same brand. Then the screen showed the tragedy of a certain man, who was in a habit of chewing large amounts of gutka—and could not be saved. As the time ticked on, so did the ads—and so did my doubts about whether the movie would finish on time.

'What will we do, just in case the movie does not finish on time?' I asked Dad.

'Whatever happens, we've to leave the mall by 6 p.m., whether the movie has finished or not. Otherwise, we may end up missing our flight,' Dad said in a determined tone.

Eventually, the time came for us to leave—around 5.45 p.m.—and let's just say that I wasn't particularly enthusiastic about leaving the movie right at its climax. Dad called our taxi driver, who said, 'I'm coming sir. Will pick you up from the same spot where I dropped you.'

Fifteen minutes passed, and there was still no sign of the driver. Dad had to call him a second time, and then a third. But the driver wasn't picking up. After about five minutes he called Dad, and said in an irritated voice, 'Sir, the parking is overcrowded, it will take a lot of time to clear up. I will come in 15–20 minutes.'

Then he disconnected the call even before Dad could

react. The three of us looked at each other and did the only thing we could do—wait.

Finally, at around 6.45 p.m., we spotted the driver racing towards us in a frantic manner. The tires screeched, the taxi halted, and out came our driver who opened the doors for us so fast that we thought his fight-or-flight mechanism had been activated.

We sat in the car and darted off towards the airport in no time. And after crossing some two or three lanes, reality hit—worse than a wrecking ball. Seemingly infinite rows and columns of cars, bikes, and buses, placed strategically on the long road, creating one of the biggest traffic jams I had ever seen. Possibly the biggest Dad had seen too, as was evident from his pale, expressionless face. Clearly, he wasn't happy seeing his carefully made calculations being dashed in the dirt by an unending array of automobiles.

'Such a foolish sentiment. I should have known better than to expect the traffic level of 2 p.m. at this time,' Dad said, in a frustrated tone.

'Will we be able to reach on time?' Mumma said.

'We just might. Even 7.30 p.m. will do—but only if this jam clears up soon.'

And of course, it didn't clear up soon. Before long, the watch showed 7.30 p.m.

'Come on man. If we maintain such a slow pace, we'll get nowhere near the airport even by 8 p.m. Driver, get this car out of this vehicular mess as soon as you can!' Dad yelled

'I am trying my level best, but looking at the traffic, the only way this car can reach the airport quickly is by flying over these vehicles. Unfortunately, as of now, it's not equipped with the necessary technology to make flight possible. So, we'll have to wait, sir,' the driver replied with an air of calmness.

No one said anything for a while after that serene verbal counterattack made by our driver. Google Maps still showed huge red lines on the road as we moved through a spectacular sea of red traffic lights. As the journey dragged on, Dad began imagining scenarios in which we might miss the flight and return as sore losers.

'What if we miss our flight?' Dad said.

'What if?' Mumma echoed.

'We would have to reschedule our entire programme from scratch.'

'When is the next flight to Singapore?'

'Not soon… not soon. What we could do is forget about this whole trip, explore New Delhi for two to three days, and go back to Dehradun,' said Dad, in a remorseless tone.

Me and Mumma decided to leave Dad to himself and not respond to his distressed remarks—he wasn't thinking clearly anymore, weighed down by the mental pressure of the delay. Eventually, Dad also succumbed to his fate and became completely silent.

At last, after narrowly escaping the traffic jam, we reached the airport—very, very late, at around 8.15 p.m. By then, I was rapidly losing all hope of our Oriental escapade getting any further. Some kind of miracle would be needed to save it now (so that you, dear reader, could read the following chapters). To be precise, the immaculately dressed, short-statured, moustache-bearing kind of miracle—who came running towards us and asked us our names.

'Travelling to Kuala Lumpur, sir?' he asked.

'Yes, we are,' Dad replied.

'Only you three are left for the check-in. Come on, we need to be quick,' he said, and waved to the curly-haired guy at the check-in counter.

By the time we reached the counter for the baggage drop, the curly-haired guy already had our freshly printed boarding passes ready. Our miracle man didn't stop here. As soon as the check-in process was complete, he led us towards the immigration counter, got our immigration forms filled, and spoke directly to the immigration officer. Because of his charisma, we weren't asked a single question—and within moments, our passports were stamped. Now, only the security check was left, but a miracle man isn't a miracle man unless he gets everything done in seconds. The security check went smoothly, and by 8.35 p.m., we found ourselves at the waiting lounges. Wonderful! We still had around 30 minutes to board the plane. That meant—even after all the hassles—we had time to refresh ourselves, grab a bite, and even do a little window shopping.

Long live the Miracle Man!

Lessons Learnt

1. A movie almost never begins at the time printed on the ticket. That window is reserved exclusively for facewash ads.
2. Age does not restrict you from seeing things with the right perspective.
3. You don't need to reach the airport two to three hours before your international flight. All you need is a Miracle Man.

Day 2

Singapore

We reached Changi airport at around 8.45 a.m. I was naturally very excited—after all, I was about to have unlimited fun over the next few days. My dream of visiting the world-famous Singapore Flyer was finally becoming a reality. I wanted to get to the hotel quickly and get some sleep before the scheduled itinerary. In fact, we all wanted some sleep. We were exhausted after the long flight, a completely sleepless night, and the jet lag.

The tour operator had arranged for a taxi that was supposed to take us to our hotel. We walked to the exit gate and started looking for someone holding a placard with our names on it. Fifteen minutes passed, and we couldn't spot any such gentleman. I was getting restless—the tiredness was mounting. Ten more minutes went by, and still no one who looked like our taxi driver could be seen. All the other passengers from our flight had already left.

Dad wanted to call the tour operator, but he didn't have a local SIM card. The Indian SIM wasn't working here. He went to a public phone and tried calling—but in vain. The public phone required coins, and Dad didn't have any. He looked helpless. This whole exercise consumed five more minutes. But then, help arrived in the form of a guy looking like a student. He saw Dad's worried face and immediately offered assistance. He handed Dad his mobile, and Dad finally managed to talk to the tour operator. The tour operator's response was as expected: 'Oh, you've already reached, and he didn't show up! He must be on his way if he hasn't arrived by now. Let me check again—I'll get back to you in a minute or two.'

'Like hell you will. I don't even have a phone,' Dad murmured to himself after the call was disconnected.

That meant we had to wait longer. Dad thanked the student-type guy, and we returned to the exit gate, exploring the idea of hiring a taxi ourselves. But for that, we would have to step out of the airport to the taxi stand. We were still deciding what to do when the student-type guy came running towards us, mobile phone in hand.

'Sir, sir—someone wants to talk to you.'

'Who might that be?'

'I think your driver.'

Dad took the phone and said something angrily. Then he disconnected the call and told us that the driver was coming in five minutes. He thanked the student-type guy again.

'Oh, you're most welcome. Is it your first time in Singapore?' he asked gently.

'Not exactly, my wife and I came here just after our marriage. My son is here for the first time,' Dad said.

'Oh nice. What's your name, buddy?' the student-type guy asked me.

'I'm Joy. You?' I replied, asking in the same breath.

'My name is Kang Young Mo.'

'Nice meeting you Kang. Are you from Singapore?'

'Well, I'm from South Korea—doing my post-graduation

at the National University of Singapore. If you get time, go and visit the University. It's worth seeing.'

So, he was a student. I patted myself on the back for identifying him as a student-type.

We chatted for a while about other places to see in Singapore. Then it was time to say goodbye. The first person I met in Singapore was such a gentleman, I thought. Suddenly, I realized that the first person I was supposed to meet in Singapore—the taxi driver—had still not arrived. Well, he wasn't proving himself to be a gentleman, was he?

We had been standing at the exit gate for almost an hour, when a short, lean man in his fifties appeared, holding a placard with our names. But there was a problem. In his other hand, he held another placard—with the names of Mrs and Mr Praveen Madaan. What did that mean? Was he here for collecting us or someone else? Mumma decided to check.

'Why are you so late?'

'Am I late ma'am? The company told me to reach here before 10.'

'Why 10? You were all aware that our flight would reach at 8.45. And what about this other placard?'

'You are two families together, right?'

'No—we don't even know anyone here.'

'Well, I was told by the company that I was to receive two families at 10 o'clock.'

We were still figuring out the equation when a newlywed couple approached us and told the driver that they were *the* Madaans we were waiting for. We boarded the taxi and started towards the hotel. Mr Madaan told us that he had come on the Air India flight that landed at 9.45 p.m.

Okay. It all became clear to us. The taxi driver was supposed to receive two families, scheduled to arrive at different times on different flights. That was why we were made to wait for one and a half hours. And it wasn't the fault of the taxi driver—the tour operators had scheduled it in such a way that they didn't have to send the car twice. How clever!

Finally, we reached our hotel, after dropping the Madaans at theirs. We were very tired and wanted to go straight to our room. But no—one more disappointment was on the way. At the reception, we were told that the check-in time at the hotel was 2 p.m. It was only 10.35 a.m.

Mumma took the lead and told the boy on the reception that we wanted to sleep straightaway. Thankfully, the receptionist was very considerate. He got a room ready in five minutes. We checked in and I hit the sack immediately.

I slept in no time. Dad woke me up when he received a call from the reception—our vehicle had arrived. It was supposed to take us to a zoo on Mandai Lake Road for the Night Safari. I was feeling fresh after a sound sleep, but it surprised me that Dad didn't sleep at all. Instead, he went to the market and purchased local SIM cards and some packets of potato wafers. Dad's managerial foresight must have warned him that I would be hungry upon waking up. Clever him.

We got ready quickly and went down to the hotel lobby, where the same driver we had met in the morning was waiting for us. He led us to a white minivan. As soon as I stepped inside, I was surprised to see the Madaan couple already seated. So, we were going to be together for the whole tour, I presumed. Not a bad idea. We'll have company. I decided to start the conversation.

'Good evening. My name is Joy.'

'Good evening. My name is Shweta and this is my husband, Praveen.'

The Madaans, I thought to myself and smiled.

'Sorry to have kept you waiting,' I said apologetically.

'Not at all. We got here just fifteen minutes ago. I was told you guys had to wait for more than an hour for us at the airport. So, we're more or less even, aren't we?'

'Come on, don't say like that. You didn't even know we were waiting—how can it be your fault? I think it is wonderful that we are grouped together for the tour. We'll enjoy it more,' Mumma intervened.

'Of course, ma'am.'

The chatting continued as we drove towards the zoo. The Madaans were very friendly. Mr Madaan told us he and his wife were software engineers, based in Bangalore. They got married recently, and this was their first trip together. I saw Mumma and Dad smiling at each other when they heard this.

I looked out of the window. Singapore was not exactly naturally beautiful, but it looked highly developed and clean. Everything seemed to be very systematic. I wondered how was it when Mumma and Dad came here after their marriage!

I was deeply engrossed in my thoughts when suddenly the driver stopped the van. Now what?

The driver went inside a hotel and—after five minutes—came out with two girls in their twenties. So, we had more company. The girls, as they told us, were from Chennai and had come here for the New Year celebration. Like all of us, they too had arrived in Singapore just today. I wondered what would have happened if their flight had arrived an hour later than the Madaans'. Maybe we'd have had to appreciate the beauty of Changi Airport for an hour more…*No, I didn't want to think about that.*

We reached the zoo at around 6.30 p.m. The minivan driver told us to be back at the pick and drop point by 10.30 p.m. in a nonchalant tone. I wondered if the Night

Safari was that long to keep us busy for four hours.

The tour operator had already provided us the entry passes for the zoo and Night Safari. We entered the zoo, and joined the long, unending queue for the Night Safari. Someone from the security staff was checking the passes. First, he went to the Madaans and found their passes to be in order. When he checked our passes, he said that since the tour operator hadn't stamped them, we couldn't use them for entry. Dad tried to explain that they had been issued like that, and now we couldn't get them stamped. The security man advised us to talk to the park manager. There was no point arguing, so we stepped out of the queue and went to the park manager. He said the same thing—the passes had to be stamped by the authorized tour operator.

Dad called the tour operator back in India. The tour operator made his boss speak to Dad—who, in turn, made his boss do the same. But it was evident from Dad's facial expressions that none of the bosses were convincing enough.

The girls from Chennai, who we had met on the van, joined us in the park manager's office. It seemed they had also booked through the same tour operator, as their tickets hadn't been stamped either. We were getting company everywhere.

Suddenly, Dad lost his temper while talking on the phone. He was very displeased with the company's attitude in the airport episode, where they cleverly made us wait for more than one hour. And now this! Dad said something very strong and effective in a language, which my 12-year-old mind could not decipher. It must've been effective because the moment Dad disconnected the call, the park manager's phone rang at full volume.

Man! It proved to be more effective than I guessed. The park manager, after talking to our tour operator in India, offered us apple juice, stamped our tickets, and escorted us to the gateway for the Night Safari. The Chennai girls were delighted. They didn't even have to say a single word to the park manager, and their problem was solved. And they got apple juice as bonus. I always suspected Dad was a magician. He knew the right *mantras,* which could be chanted to make someone do the needful. I wished I could learn all his tricks when I grow up.

We reached the Night Safari gate, and found that the queue had become considerably longer than the last time we had been a part of it. I was in the process of calculating how much time we would take to reach somewhere near the entry gate when Mr Madaan came to our rescue. He took us to the front of the queue, where Mrs Madaan was waiting for us.

Apparently, they had told the people just behind them that the seven of us were together and that originally, all of us were standing in that part of the queue. Strangely, no one seemed to mind, and they made place for us. The Madaans were turning out to be really sweet and caring. Well, the fact that we had been forced to wait for the Madaans at the airport was not hurting me anymore.

The Night Safari was wonderful, and I, for the first time, saw animals like lions, tigers, and hyenas living in the open. Our group of seven took the same cart on the safari train and enjoyed each other's company. For the first time since I had landed in Singapore, I was properly feeling good.

The long struggle to get an entry to the safari, a very long queue, and the safari itself had been exhausting, and it made us feel hungry. Since there was no possibility of getting any vegetarian fare at our hotel, we decided to look for something in the zoo campus itself. The Chennai girls were also looking for vegetarian food, so we stopped at an Indian vegetarian stall. Since the Madaans had their dinner included in their tour package, they didn't stop for food and went to the souvenir shop instead.

It was already 10.30 p.m. when we finished eating. We rushed to the exit gate where the van driver was supposed to meet us. We had barely reached the gate when we saw our van leaving. I caught a glimpse of Mrs Madaan sitting in the front seat, saying something to the driver. It looked as if she was arguing over something. Soon enough, the van left the scene.

It was very disappointing for us—it was our first day here, and we had already so many bad experiences. We considered taking a public bus, but we hardly had any idea of the routes.

The magician in Dad came alive again. He called the tour operator in India once more. This time, he sounded very calm. I heard him speaking in a composed tone.

'See dear, this is the third time in a day we are having problems because of you. You made us wait at the airport, then you caused us problems in the safari by not stamping our tickets. Now, because of you, we got a late entry in the safari, and that caused the slight delay in us reaching the exit gate at 10.30 sharp. Dear friend, call the van driver immediately. Tell him to come back here and pick us up. AM I MAKING MYSELF CLEAR?'

And he disconnected the phone. Six minutes and thirty-seven seconds later, the van was there to pick us. The Chennai girls were looking at Dad in disbelief. I smiled at Mumma. This was no surprise to us. We had seen Dad speaking in a cold and determined voice, and getting things done countless times. In the van, Mumma thanked Mrs Madaan. She had seen us at the gate and told the driver to wait for us, but he wouldn't listen. Now, after everything, we were in a cheerful mood and laughed our hearts out about the van driver and the tour operator.

Lessons Learnt

1. The first person you meet at the beginning of your intercontinental voyage might be a gentleman. In the words of Paulo Coelho, *beginner's luck!*
2. Never, ever trust tour operators completely—no matter how grand their promises may be.
3. Always have a plan B ready—just in case.

Day 3

Singapore

The phone in the hotel room rang and woke me up. I was the nearest to it, so I felt the moral obligation to take it.

'Hello!'

'Good morning, sir! I'm speaking from the reception, your pick up is waiting in the lobby.'

'What time is it?'

'It's 7 in the morning.'

'Okay, tell the driver to wait.'

I analysed the situation. Even after a monolithic sleep, I was not feeling fresh. Last night, we came back to the hotel at around 11.30. By the time we managed to hit the sack, it was well past midnight. In fact, I didn't want to go anywhere so early in the morning. Mumma and Dad would have been feeling the same, I guessed. But if we didn't take the van now, we were going to miss the whole itinerary for today.

I woke Dad up and explained the situation to him. Dad, in turn, woke Mumma up and asked her to get ready in ten minutes. From her expression, I could tell Mumma didn't seem very much interested in the proposition of getting ready on such a short notice—given how draining the previous day had been. Mumma asked me if I would be good to go in five minutes. I looked at Dad's face. He asked Mumma to decide quickly. Finally, it was agreed that none of us were ready to get out of bed.

The phone rang again. Dad answered it this time—it was the van driver calling from the lobby. Dad listened patiently and, in the end, told him to enjoy his free day. We went back to sleep and woke up again at 9.15 a.m.

When we finally got ready to start our day, it was somewhere around 11.30. Since we had to plan our day ourselves, it was left to me to decide on the places we were going to.

We started with the Singapore Flyer, the second tallest Ferris wheel in the world. It's a gigantic observation wheel with 28 city-bus-sized, air-conditioned capsules. We sat in one of them, and the wheel started moving at a gentle pace. After around fifteen minutes, our capsule reached the top. The view from the top was spectacular.

As I was looking out of the capsule glass, an old man came near me, gave a vibrant smile, and said hello. It was third or fourth time since I landed in Singapore that a stranger approached and started talking to me like that.

Although my parents never told me that, but I had always read it in the dos and don'ts section of travel guides that kids should not talk to strangers. And despite having better shopping skills than Dad, and being more tech-savvy than mom, I was technically still a kid. Somehow, I couldn't resist the urge to talk to a local and decided to strike up a brief conversation.

'Hello!' I smiled back.

'Do you know how tall is this flyer?' The old man was still smiling.

'Yeah, its 165 metres. I read it on a sign in the boarding hall.'

'And how tall is 165 metres?'

'Very, very tall, I presume.'

'Imagine 32 giraffes stacked on top of one another.'

My eyes widened. The old man was now smiling ear to ear. He knew now was the perfect time to load me with some more information.

'See, young man, this is the beautiful city of Singapore in its full glory. There is the Merlion, spouting water into the river, and these buildings here are the Esplanade – Theatres on the Bay. Can you see those three tall buildings connected at the top by a boat-like structure?'

'Yes, of course.'

'That is Marina Bay Sands hotel.'

Looks like cricket stumps, I thought to myself. The old man seemed to know everything. By the time we came down after a full circle, he had already enlightened me about every corner of the city. I wondered if he came to the flyer every day, made friends with kids, and disseminated his knowledge for free.

We were very hungry by the time we came out of the flyer complex. We looked for snack shops nearby, but again, being vegetarian limited our options. At one corner of the street, there was an Indian-looking snack bar. We went straight to it. The vendor was a Chinese and it turned out he didn't have anything that contained animal products. Although he had small and tapered *samosas*, which he claimed to be filled with vegetables, we decided to keep away from them. The *vegetarian* samosas were not looking vegetarian enough to satisfy our vegetarian needs. But the vendor proved to be helpful—if not with his food, then at least with his piece of advice.

'If you want *Jain* vegetarian food, you can go to *Little India*.'

'What exactly is *Jain* vegetarian food?' I couldn't keep myself from asking. The vendor stared at me as if I had asked something very foolish. Mumma came to my rescue by answering my question.

'It is a type of vegetarian food that doesn't contain onions or garlic.'

'But why would we avoid eating onions and garlic? They are vegetables, aren't they?'

'Forget it, Joy. Let's get going.'

'Where to? Little India? But I don't reckon avoiding onions or garlic is on my to-do list.'

'Okay fine. That was funny. Now can we go?'

We took a taxi and went to Little India. It is a colourful and vibrant area on Serangoon Road, full of Indian shops, temples, and—of course—migrants. Seeing so many shops around freshened Mumma's mood. But eating something was our first priority, so we entered a South Indian restaurant.

A manager-type staff member, clad in South Indian-style *lungi* welcomed us and guided us towards a sitting area just in front of the reception. Just as I sat there, I realized the sofa had no accompanying table. Before I could say anything, the 'manager-type' lungi-clad staff member said something—most likely to himself—pointing towards the eating area. I couldn't understand his thick Tamil accent.

'Are you saying something?' Mom asked him.

'Yes ma'am. You will have to wait for five to ten minutes,' he replied. Mumma and Dad looked at each other, as if contemplating the option of going to some other restaurant. But the manager-type staff member went on with his South Indian-sounding speech: 'Ma'am, sir, this is the busiest restaurant in the whole Little India. It is almost always full. Not only South Indians, but also North Indians—and even the locals—come here. We serve the best Tamil rice meal. The locals here love our special *thali.* You know, some time back, the Prime Minister of India also came and had lunch here. In fact, we only use the best spices imported straight from India.'

He went on and on until one of the tables was vacant and a waiter took us in. I kept wondering whether the duty of this 'manager type' guy was to engage people in conversation while they waited for the table.

We walked to our table, ordered and waited. After two to three minutes, the same 'manager type' guy escorted another Indian family and seated them next to us. The man was speaking incessantly, while his wife listened patiently. Their little girl, as soon as she got a place to sit, became busy playing games on her mother's mobile. From their conversation, I quickly gathered that they lived in Singapore. The couple appeared highly educated, and much of their conversation revolved around their Filipino maid.

I didn't mean to eavesdrop on their nonstop chitchat, but the man was speaking so loudly that all the guests in the restaurant, who understood either Hindi or English knew—within 10 minutes—that their maid ran away with her belongings, without informing them. On top of that the maid placement agency was apparently not serious about their problem.

The wife had applied for a leave from her office, which was turned down by her boss. She was pregnant too, so she couldn't do any heavy work. The husband had applied for leave from his university, where he taught Nuclear Physics, and his leave was sanctioned. And here he was—managing the household, the little girl's homework, and the pregnant wife's daily chores.

His new research paper was long overdue, but he wasn't getting any time to finish it. If he had known this was going to happen, he would never have come from Patna to Singapore. And if he had known that dealing with his Tamil-speaking daughter was going to be so difficult, he would never have married a girl from Madurai.

The waiter brought our meals. I had ordered idlis and vadas, while Dad and Mumma went for Tamil rice meals. We had just started eating when the vocal man sitting next to us turned towards me and asked in his loud voice,

'Joy, which school in Dehradun you go to?'

And I was like—how on earth could he know my name and my city! It was me who should have known everything about him, because he was speaking nonstop—and definitely not the other way round. He must have had wonderful ears, because even when his mouth was in continuous motion, his ears managed to hear Dad or Mumma calling me by name. Pure genius, I deduced.

'You are Joy, right? My name is Mahesh Rai,' he said.

I was about to answer when I felt the 'stranger alert' coming from somewhere. Every time a stranger approached me, I received this alert from my subconscious mind that I, being a kid, should not talk to strangers. And every time I ignored this alert. So, this time it shouldn't be any different, I told myself.

Moreover, was this man really a stranger? I knew he was from Patna, India. I knew he was teaching in a university, he was about to finish his research paper in Nuclear Physics, he married a woman from Madurai—who was guilty of speaking to their daughter in Tamil. I also knew that his Filipino maid ran away. The only thing I hadn't known so far was his name, which he had just told. So, even if talking to strangers was not advisable for kids, this man didn't fall into the category of strangers at all. I smiled at him, and decided to offer my hand of friendship.

'Hi Mr Rai. You already know my name.'

'You're here on vacation?'

'Yes, sir!'

Then I formally introduced him to my parents—whose name he most probably already knew. I told him the name of my school, and wondered what would he do with this wonderful piece of information. He formally introduced us to his wife, as if we already didn't know that her name was Kavitha, and she was from Madurai. By the time the introduction part was over, we had finished the meals, and it was time to go back to the hotel.

Mr Rai then asked for Dad's mobile number in India. I had a hunch that he was just being polite; in fact, he already knew Dad's number. And everything else about us. Whatever.

Since we had slept well last night, we were still feeling fresh. So, we decided to make the most of the time we had. In no time, we found ourselves at the Singapore River, where a boat tour was waiting for us. Well—not exactly waiting for us—as we had to wait in a queue briefly for our turn. Mumma was looking excited. But I admit, I was a bit worried. What if this was one of those 'boring historical' tours, where you have to pretend to be interested? However, all my worries were gone the moment our boat captain introduced himself to us.

'Hi sir! Hello ma'am! My name is Wei. I'm your boat captain and tour guide. I'm like a software update—you don't always know when I'll show up. But when I do, I promise I'll make things a little more interesting!' he said cheerfully.

So, we were in for a treat. This guy wasn't just your average, boring tour guide. It seemed that the tour was going to be fun. The tour started with Clarke Quay. Wei didn't miss a chance to sound interesting. 'Guys, this is Clarke Quay. People from all over the world come here to be a part of an eternal celebration. Here the only thing more colourful than the buildings is the cocktails.'

At every stop, Wei would begin by giving us the lowdown on the history of the place. But then, just when you thought it was going to get all serious and lecture-y, he would throw in a line that had us all in stitches. When we passed by the Merlion statue, Wei's eyes blinked.

'Sir, this is Merlion, a mythical creature that symbolizes the city's origin as a fishing village.'

'Is it a fish? It looks more like lion,' I chipped in.

'Oh sir, it is fifty per cent lion, fifty per cent fish, and one hundred per cent guaranteed to make your Instagram photos look exotic.'

We all laughed, but Dad remained serious. Then we passed by another landmark. The Fullerton Hotel.

'This is a grand historical building that was once the General Post Office. It's now a luxury hotel. The rooms here are so luxurious, even the pillows deserve a spa day.'

This time, even Dad couldn't help smiling, but apparently, he gave Wei that look: half *That's a good one*, and half *I'm too mature for this nonsense*. And the tour continued, with a balanced mix of historical knowledge and spot-on punchlines.

Now, after having several great experiences in one day, I was not at all upset about missing the organized group trip. In fact, I felt like we had won a lottery. Not only I got to enjoy a ride in the Singapore Flyer, I was also introduced to the magical abilities of Mr Rai at the restaurant. And finally, this almost private river safari, where I got to experience the night view of the sights with some top-notch humour sprinkled in.

Lessons Learnt

1. Talking to strangers is not always bad. Even if it is, you can't always avoid it.
2. Be prepared to spend fifty per cent of your time looking for an Indian vegetarian restaurant if you are vegetarian. Make it seventy-five if you're looking for 'Jain' vegetarian cuisine.
3. A maid is always a precious commodity for Indians; doesn't matter in which part of the universe they live in.
4. Tour guides are not always dull. Some of them are encyclopaedias with a punchline.

Day 4

Singapore

My excitement knew no bounds. After all, today was going to be filled with adventures. We were going to Universal Studios and other attractions of Sentosa Island, and without doubt I was going to have some of the most magical experiences in the world. The pickup was supposed to arrive at 9, but I got up at 7, and somehow convinced my parents to grab an early breakfast. Of course, early by our standards!

After breakfast, I went back to the hotel room and started preparing my day bag for the trip to Sentosa. By the time Mumma and Dad reached the room, I was completely ready. I instructed them to get ready quickly, and ran down to the hotel lobby. While it was only 8.45, my excitement was rising, and I was looking at my Casio Pro Trek wristwatch every two minutes. Dad and Mumma came down together at 8.55. Dad smiled and said, 'It seems that the driver is going to be late today, when we are on time.'

'Dad, I hope he's not late, at least not today,' I said

'We still have a couple of minutes. He'll come,' Dad replied.

The moment Dad said this, a bundle of energy in the form of a short heighted woman burst through the lobby door with a poor looking guy in tow. She had a placard in her hands, with our names written on it. Wow! This woman was like walking sunshine, all smiles and bubbly vibes.

When we saw the placard, we approached her and introduced ourselves.

'Hi! My name is Queeny. I'm your tour guide. *Chalo*.' She shook our hands in a cheerful way, and guided us towards the door. Then she turned to the poor looking man behind her, who probably was the cab driver, and said,

'Start the bus, hero. Chalo, Chalo.'

'Is it a bus, Queeny?' Mom asked.

'Yes sweetheart, a bus. There are eight more people we have to pick. Now chalo.'

'From this hotel?' Mumma asked.

'No, from different hotels,' Queeny replied.

'That would take time,' Mumma said.

'Yes, that's why I'm saying chalo.' Queeny laughed heartily.

'One hour?' Mom tried to clarify.

'Maybe more than that. Chalo, Chalo. We've to reach Mount Faber cable car station at eleven,' Queeny said.

'Eleven? That means we're not going to Sentosa directly?' I was disappointed.

'Well, baby, we have to collect others too. Trust me, you're not going to miss anything.' Queeny tried to convince me.

'Queeny, when we've almost two hours with us, why don't you drop us at Chinatown, then pick us up again.' It was Mumma again.

'Oh, dear madam, would have loved to, but you know, there are going to be others on the cab, and they might object, so not possible, Chalo, Chalo.'

One thing was sure. Queeny had a thing for Hindi. And by '*thing*' I mean her one-word vocabulary, *Chalo*. I mean seriously! She could give any parrot a run for its money with that level of repetition. I was still trying to piece together what exactly *chalo* meant in Queeny's universe when I heard Mumma's proposal.

'Okay, tell you what, you go ahead and pick your other guests up. We can't waste two hours waiting, so we're going to Chinatown. We will do some shopping over there and meet you at the cable car station at eleven,' Mumma said.

Queeny was shocked at Mumma's proposal. Or so she appeared to be. She said in a concerned voice:

'Sweet lady, it is not advisable to shop alone in Chinatown. It's very dangerous.'

'Dangerous? What could be dangerous in a shopping place?' Mumma asked.

'The street vendors in Chinatown are very smart and cunning, they quote very high prices. If you are not a local, they would charge a lot of money from you. You would be literally cheated there, chalo.'

'Oh, don't you worry dear. All the markets in the world are the same. You should have confidence in your bargaining skills, and no one can cheat you.' Mumma said.

'As you wish. Chalo,' Queeny said.

'We'll just do a little shopping, have some snacks if we feel like it, and that's all. See you at Mount Faber. Keep our cable car tickets ready,' Mumma said.

So, we laughed it off, reassured Queeny that we have got it under control, and headed off to the land of street vendors—Chinatown. Who knows, maybe we'll come back with a tale of a successful bargain.

Chinatown street market is one of the most popular spots in Singapore for people with my mom's flair for bargaining. Small shops and stalls line entire streets, including Pagoda

Street, Trengganu Street, Sago Lane, Smith Street, and Temple Street.

We started walking from one end and I was surprised to see that most of the street was rather empty. Mom asked one of the locals, and was told that most shops open after ten. Obviously, we had around half an hour in our pocket to do a market survey before Mumma tried her luck with her bargaining skills.

The food carts at Smith Street were open though, but for us, it was nothing to be excited about, because almost all of them were selling non-vegetarian things. Moreover, we had just had breakfast at the hotel, so we weren't exactly starving. As we moved through the market, more and more shops began to open. Within minutes, the whole market was bustling with the enthusiastic voices of shopkeepers trying to tempt us just to check out their wares.

It was hardly surprising that most of the stalls were selling similar types of souvenirs. These ranged from waving lucky cats to impressive lacquerware and handmade cane and palm items decorated with calligraphy. This all made Mumma's mood very fresh. She started looking for something for the family.

'Mumma, are you taking something from here, or just window shopping?' I couldn't keep myself from asking.

'I want a waving cat. It brings luck, they say.'

'Yeah, take one. Maybe it'll improve our luck with the tour operators,' Dad said, smiling.

Then we saw a very big gift shop. It seemed they had all sorts of Chinese souvenirs you could think of. The name of the shop was also very interesting—*The Gift Shop*. Very innovative, I thought. I wanted to go in, as the toy section looked bigger than Hamleys. But Mumma had other ideas.

She was of the firm opinion that big shops leave no scope for bargaining.

'But, at the same time, their prices are quite reasonable. On the other hand, the street vendors quote very high prices, don't they?' said Dad.

'Yes, they do. But, what else am I there for?'

So, it had to be a street vendor.

We stopped at a small stall, owned by a smiling man in his fifties. Mumma selected a fortune cat and asked its price.

'Hello, madam, my name is Li, and my shop is the oldest in the market. This is the best cat you will get in the whole market. And its size too is perfect, so you can carry it with you wherever you go. I say madam, you take it, price is no issue.' The shopkeeper said and started wrapping the lucky cat in brown paper.

'Oh wait, sir! Tell me the price first.' Mumma insisted.

'Price is no issue madam, as I said. I will give you the best price in the market. Have I ever overcharged the customers, Xiang?' He now addressed the girl who was helping him. The girl smiled.

'Mr Li, we don't have all day. Tell me the price.'

'If you say so. The normal price is 60 dollars but since you're my first customer today, you just give 55.' When he said this, I noticed an overfriendly, *ah-another-brave-soul-to-outwit-me-in-the-art-of-bargaining* smile plastered on his face.

'Mr Li, I will give you 10 dollars for this,' Mumma said in a firm tone. Definitely, she was not a newbie in the art of bargaining. She was like a warrior on a mission, armed with nothing but her wits and a fierce determination to save a few bucks.

'Sorry madam. I'll give it to my grandson to play instead.

Even I paid more than double of what you're saying. I tell you, just give 50 and this lucky charm is yours.'

'10.'

'Alright, 45.'

'10.'

'Madam, if you don't want to take this piece, I can show you some cheaper ones. But this one will not be less than 45,' he said and picked up an almost similar piece from the shop.

'How much for this?'

'This one is 25 dollars.'

Mumma looked closely at both the pieces as if she was trying to find out the difference between them. They looked totally similar. She instantly sensed that the shopkeeper was trying to finalize the sale by showing two pieces of the same make at different prices, and now was the time to close the deal.

'Mr Li, I'll take the first piece for 10 dollars.'

'Not possible madam.' Lee shook his head.

'Thank you for your time, sir. We'll take it from some other shop. Let's go Joy.' Mumma and Dad started to leave the shop.

'Madam, listen. You're my first customer today. Come back, I'll give you the first piece at 20 dollars.' Li was now quoting a much better price.

'See, I can give you 15 tops. Not a single penny more.' Mumma exactly knew how much would be a reasonable price.

'Fine madam. 15 it is. Xiang, pack the lucky cat. And don't forget to keep an extra pair of cells.'

The girl began following the instructions and then handed the packet to Mumma. Finally, after what felt like an eternity of negotiations, Mumma emerged victorious, clutching her prized fortune cat like it was the holy grail.

'Li, this pretty girl is your daughter?'

'Yes madam. We live nearby. Would you care to visit our place?'

'Oh, thank you so much, Li. We are running short of time. Maybe someday I'll come with more time on my hands, and then I'll visit your place.'

'But I must say, your son looks very bright,' Li said with all seriousness. I was taken aback. Where did that come from? Dad too was surprised when he said that. He asked, 'How could you tell that, Li? You've barely seen him for ten to fifteen minutes. And you didn't even talk to him.'

'I am an old man, sir. These eyes have seen all types of people. Your son was observing each and everything. He was, like, taking notes of your wife's conversation with me. Come here, son.'

I went to shake his hands, still in a state of shock as if this wily shopkeeper had caught me doing something. But Li—very gently—touched my forehead and said in a calm manner, 'I want to give you some Japanese wisdom. *Nana korobi ya oki.* Fall down seven times, stand up eight. My son, this timeless proverb embodies the resilience and perseverance deeply ingrained in oriental culture. It reminds us that setbacks are inevitable in life; however, true strength lies in our ability to rise each time we stumble. So remember, no matter how many times we may fall, we should always have the power to stand up again, stronger and wiser.'

My surprise level increased. How come this old shopkeeper—trying to take home some extra bucks from us some time back—was so calm and composed when he started sharing this excellent piece of wisdom! Incredible. Dad and Mom were speechless too.

I thanked Li profoundly. Aryan was right. I was certainly learning new things. We said goodbye to the shopkeeper and took a taxi to Mount Faber, where we had to meet Queeny for further activities of the day. I remained silent during the ten to twelve-minute taxi ride. Li's words were still echoing in my mind.

We were greeted by none other than the *chalo* queen at the entrance of Mount Faber. She guided us to the cable car terminal atop a building by saying endless chalos, and handed us the tickets. We were disappointed to see the unbelievably long queue for the ride, and it was moving at a snail's pace. Queeny seated us on some waiting chairs with other guests from our group. Dad asked, 'Queeny, will this take long?'

'No, sir, we are a group of 12, including me. We'll be booked in two cars at the same time. In ten to fifteen minutes, we'll start. Let me talk to the officials,' Queeny said and left the scene.

All of us kept waiting for almost half an hour. Our sincere group guide didn't come back. Nor could we manage to get a seat in the cable car. I started feeling hungry. There were a couple of well decorated restaurants on the same floor. When we felt that Queeny was taking a lifetime to come back, we went to one of the vegetarian restaurants and ordered a veg sandwich.

Ten minutes passed. I was starving and there was no sign of my sandwich. The anticipation started killing me. I decided to ask the waiter.

'Sir, what happened to my sandwich?'

'Coming sir—very soon,' he replied in a robotic voice.

Five more minutes passed. As the minutes were ticking by, I started wondering if whether they were growing the veggies themselves.

Eventually, I started to panic as we had the cable car to catch. But just as I was about to go full karen on the waiter,

Dad's phone rang. It was Queeny, asking us to come back to the cable car terminal immediately. We didn't think twice and dashed out of the restaurant quickly.

At the terminal, we saw that our car was ready to depart, with Queeny and two elderly passengers already inside. One part of the group had likely left earlier. We boarded the beautifully decorated trolley and began our ride to Sentosa Island. The elderly people, as it turned out, were a French couple—Mr and Mrs Garnier. The name instantly hit me—Garnier.

The cable car was remarkably comfortable. It had flip seats and a music system. And the view was spectacular! Queeny pointed out Resorts World Sentosa's adventure cove, lush jungle foliage, and the surrounding coastline. She gave a beautiful description of each location. She told us about the S.E.A. Aquarium, the Wings of Time show, and other attractions we were going to see—Sentosa's evolution into a world class tourist destination, and its dark history during the Second World War. She also described the rides we were going to experience at Universal Studios, and numerous dining options available across the island.

Wait! What, eat? I suddenly remembered the sandwich I ordered. What would have happened to it? I mean seriously, would it still be sitting there on a plate, feeling neglected and abandoned, just like my appetite? Or they never prepared it at all! If they actually did, I couldn't help but imagine the poor waiter scratching his head, wondering where the heck we disappeared. Maybe he served the sandwich to someone else, a hero, a sandwich saviour who stumbled upon our abandoned order and gave it the love and attention it deserved. Or maybe it's still there, a monument of our impatience.

And the most chilling thing was the feeling that we'll never ever know about the fate of that sandwich. Whatever.

Finally, we arrived at Sentosa—the place where children's dreams come true and parents' wallets beg for mercy. We began with Universal Studios, followed by other attractions across the island, after lunch. It turned out that we were the only ones in the group to go to Universal Studios; the others, including the French couple, were going to other places in Sentosa.

Universal Studios Singapore is definitely one of the places every fun-loving person should visit at least once in their lifetime—it is basically a battlefield for your adrenaline, candy for your eyes, and occasionally, a strong test of your iron will.

Queeny guided us through the entrance of Universal Studios, and informed that we had to join the group again before 2.30 p.m. That meant we could only fit about four or five rides in our tight schedule as it was already 11.40 a.m. We had the tickets, along with other essentials. So, we marched right through the gates without delaying any further.

The first activity we did there was a well-known 'ritual' that every person with a camera on their phone follows—a family photo at the iconic Universal Studios Globe. Once that was done, we headed to our first ride of the day—the *Battlestar Galactica*: *Human vs. Cylon*. For the first time on this trip, something was going according to plan, without any unnecessary delays. Right?

The sight of the overcrowded queue gave me a strange feeling of déjà vu, reminding me of the titanic traffic jam we faced back in New Delhi on the way to the airport. The only difference was that here, the automobiles were replaced by long rows of tourists. After some time, it turned out that there was one more difference. We didn't have any miracle man here.

After half an hour of standing in the long queue, and

absorbing a week's worth of Vitamin D, I saw some people getting on the same ride as us, without having to spend a minute waiting in the queue. When I told Dad about this sorcery, it visibly piqued his interest. The prospect of cutting straight through the queues to get to the good part sure sounded nice. In fact, it was absolutely necessary at the moment, considering the fact that we only had about two and a half hours in our hands to join Queeny and others.

'Excuse me, why do the people over there not have to wait in the line for their turn?' Dad enquired with a staff member, gesturing towards the second entrance.

'No line for them, sir. They have express passes to skip the wait. The others, including you, have ordinary passes, and have to wait for your turn, sir,' the staff member replied.

I can only guess, but Dad must have recalled the entire Madaan episode, thinking to himself, 'Our crooked tour operators have fooled us yet again by not mentioning a single thing about Express passes.'

'Well, where can I get them? And, do I've to pay for the tickets all over again?'

'You can get them at the ticket counter, sir. And no, you won't have to buy new tickets. Express passes are just add-ons you can buy any time to upgrade your existing tickets.'

Dad thanked the staff member for the helpful information, rushed to the ticket counter, and got our tickets upgraded with express pass add-ons—a smart move. With our newfound powers of legally cutting lines, we headed towards our first ride, which was of course, the *Battlestar Galactica* roller coaster.

Right off the bat, we knew that this was no ordinary coaster. It started off slow but got *unbelievably* fast—reaching around ninety kilometres per hour in a matter of seconds. The combination of speed, terrifying power, and a disorienting array of twists and turns was an experience even seasoned riders would fear.

The coaster delivered rapid twisted drops, exciting laterals, and looped around the track for some time before doing something I was, frankly, not ready for. The car took a 180-degree vertical turn, completely inverting itself and us with it, leaving us with a view of the ground. With a high-speed turn, the track ascended into a sweeping G-force curve before entering the final lateral ahead of the brake run. As the car hit the brakes, they tightened with impressive force and speed, bringing the train to a somewhat smooth stop. The exhilarating ride left Dad with a lasting motion sickness, acrophobia, and me, a newfound respect for solid ground.

Then we headed straight to the *Transformers* ride. I had no idea what to expect, but Dad didn't seem eager to join us—I knew that. To be honest, I don't blame him. Anyone with a dislike for fast rides would do the same, especially after riding a roller coaster like that. But he came along after a little persuasion from Mumma. Now I had the task of not letting Dad scream louder than me. As it was, I failed miserably.

We joined *Optimus Prime and the Autobots* as freedom fighters in the war to save humanity from the villainous *Decepticons* as they invaded the *NEST Headquarters*. We raced through the virtual city, zipping through subway tunnels, along streets and across high-rise rooftops, destroying some annoying bots along the way. Honestly speaking, for a ride that only used a pair of 3D glasses and occasional atmospheric theatrics, it was absolutely marvellous. Definitely much better than the '7D rides' and 'VR shows' back in Dehradun. And thankfully, this ride was free of motion sickness, which meant I could take Dad with me to the next ride too.

Next up was the *Jurassic Park Rapids Adventure.* We quickly got seated in a circular raft and were pushed down the white-water raft system. Our wild ride through the waterways of *Jurassic Park* had officially begun, and it was replete with tons of movie-accurate dinosaurs, and the iconic *InGen Headquarters* buildings. The first prehistoric creature that we encountered was an overly small Dilophosaurus which welcomed us by spraying us in the face. How rude! Not all dinosaurs were overly small though, as we watched some of the larger sauropods like Apatosaurus grazing on their preferred kinds of flora. The climax began after a thrilling white-water drop, when the fan favourite theropod, Tyrannosaurus rex, chased us through a dark tunnel, seeking its next meal. The circular raft was being tossed around the water as we attempted to avoid being lunch.

Now, we were ready for the last ride of the day, *Revenge of the Mummy.* This one was an indoor roller coaster ride into the total darkness of a pharaoh's tomb. Relative to the previous rides, it had a much more creepily designed interior, which made the atmosphere all the more eerie. The cart we were seated in was surrounded on all sides by huge fireballs, swarms of scarab beetles, and an army of cursed warrior mummies, all appearing from the darkness, out of nowhere. And if that was not enough, strange, pseudo-human screams could be heard in the distance every time the cart made a turn. Ancient Egyptian zombies would jump-scare you when you least expected it. Finally, Imhotep, the pharaoh himself, appeared and said something in ancient Egyptian that no one could understand. In all likelihood, he wanted us to 'return the slab'.

Queeny's deadline was nearing, so we grabbed a quick lunch and ran to the Universal Studio gift shop, where Mumma spent a lot of Singapore dollars on buying *Minion* plushies for every kid in our extended family back in India.

Then at sharp 2.30 p.m., we rejoined our group. Now, in the second innings, the first place we were supposed to go was S.E.A. Aquarium. Our chalo queen gave us a few directions.

'Mr and Mrs Garnier, you will be with master Joy and his parents. See, we'll go to AdventureLand at 4 p.m. When you're done with the aquarium, give me a call and wait for me at the exit gate. I'll come.'

'Oh, do not worry, Queeny dear. I'm old and experienced enough to guide this young family. This family is mine now. Plus, I've to take some information about the *Transformer* ride from this young kid.' Monsieur Garnier shook his head and assured Queeny.

We went inside the aquarium. It was like stepping into an underwater wonderland, where the sea creatures were the stars, and we were the paparazzi. There are more than thousand species of aquatic animals there, including the majestic Manta rays, playful dolphins, and jellyfish that glowed like night lights.

Our group had its charm too. After all, we had Monsieur and Mademoiselle Garnier with us. They added a certain *je ne sais quoi* to the underwater experience. I jokingly said to Monsieur Garnier, 'You know, your name is very popular in India.'

'Oh yes, little boy, I do. In fact, I'm very famous among the people who care for their hair. Everywhere in the world.' He quickly understood that I was referring to the *Garnier* hair care products.

'But kid, you might not be knowing one interesting thing about my husband,' Mademoiselle Garnier said it with a touch of tongue-in-cheek humour.

'Tell me, madame.'

'Monsieur Garnier is somehow convinced that every creature in this world is an old friend. Wait until you see him talking to those poor marine animals,' she laughed.

'They actually are. I can understand and speak their language. When my wife makes fun of them, those animals are not very happy,' Monsieur Garnier clarified.

'She makes fun of them?' I was curious.

'She mimics them. And they aren't happy.'

'And how do you know they aren't happy?' I asked.

'They tell me,' replied Monsieur Garnier.

'Like, you know their language?' I asked again.

'Umm, it's mostly through brainwaves,' Monsieur Garnier replied.

So, the old Frenchman did talk to the animals. Or he believed he did.

'I'll show you,' he said and tapped on the glass. One octopus swam up close. He called out a name that sounded suspiciously like that of a famous French philosopher and whispered something near the glass. The octopus darted away.

'What happened to it, sir?'

'I told it that my wife is going to be rude to them again, and it has gone to tell others,' he said very sincerely.

Meanwhile, I noticed that Mademoiselle Garnier was surrounded by a group of school-going children. They were laughing while she was doing a surprisingly accurate stingray impression that had children and adults alike in stiches. So, Monsieur Garnier was not wrong. To amuse the fellow travellers, she was annoying the sea creatures. I wanted to see Mumma's reaction but she was busy on her phone. Maybe she knew that the French couple were just making all of us enjoy the visit.

Throughout the visit, Monsieur and Mademoiselle kept

on entertaining other tourists. Everyone was laughing and enjoying the great French company. Dad too was laughing heartily when Monsieur tried to engage a particularly stoic sea turtle in a deep philosophical discussion by calling it Alexander. The sea turtle seemed fixed in place.

We were near the exit now, and it was time to leave for other adventures. Mumma, however, didn't seem as excited.

'Mumma, is there a problem?' I asked.

'Yes, baby. There is no signal on the mobile,' she said in a serious voice. I looked around for Dad. He was trying to locate Queeny. In fact, Queeny wasn't at the place where she was supposed to meet us, and no one in our group had any mobile connectivity. I was thinking of suggesting Monsieur Garnier to use his brainwaves to connect to Queeny. But who knows, his brainwaves worked only with marine animals.

I was getting restless, as it was almost 4 o'clock, and I didn't want to miss the adventures of the mysterious island. Dad and Monsieur Garnier decided to check nearby restaurants. And, bingo—there she was. Just when despair was about to set in, we spotted our gorgeous guide. She was sitting in an Indian restaurant, calmly sipping lassi.

'*Chalo*!' she exclaimed upon seeing us, as if we had been the ones who had disappeared. We could only laugh—partly out of relief and partly out of the absurdity of it all.

Queeny had everything impeccably organized. She had the tickets ready, and we were ushered into the *Journey 2: The Mysterious Island* show.

The show was a riot. We were tossed around in our seats like popcorn in a kettle. The special effects made it feel like the islanders were about to start charging us rent. Mumma seemed to be particularly enjoying herself. Every time a virtual boulder narrowly missed us, she probably relished the thought of how many calories she was burning from sheer fright. Monsieur Garnier was very quiet though. At each twist and turn, he looked like he was reconsidering every life choice that led him to this moment. Madame Garnier clutched her purse, as if fearing that a virtual pterodactyl might swoop down and snatch it away.

After surviving the virtual perils of the mysterious island, we made our way to Fort Siloso Skywalk. It was here that our French comrades staged a dignified retreat. They decided to wait for us outside.

'But I've taken tickets for you two. It will be wasted,' Queeny asked Monsieur Garnier.

'No issues, Queeny dear. We've had enough adventures. Let these young people enjoy themselves,' he replied in a cool manner.

'But you'll love it.'

'I'm loving it here. I've no intention of defying gravity on a contraption like this,' Monsieur declared, channelling his inner philosopher.

So, it was decided that the Garniers will enjoy the solid ground and recount tales of more horizontal experiences. I had a suspicion that some marine creature had telepathically warned Monsieur Garnier against this aerial escapade. Perhaps a jellyfish with a knack of telepathy.

The skywalk was exhilarating, offering panoramic views that made me feel on top of the world. As the sun at Sentosa began to set, we made our way to the grand finale, the *Wings of Time* show, a great spectacle of water, light, and pyrotechnics. With music playing in the background, lasers slicing through the night, and fountains of water dancing in sync, it was absolutely satisfying to the eyes.

Despite the minor hiccups and a trailer of the French

rebellion at the skywalk, the day was filled with unforgettable moments. It was a delightful mix of thrill, humour, and the kind of peculiar charm that only your family, an overexcited guide, express passes, and slightly bewildered French friends can bring.

Lessons Learnt

1. When life gives you Queeny and her trusty *chalo*, you roll with it. She knows what she's doing.
2. Shopping is no fun until you're forced to haggle the price down.
3. Never order a vegetarian sandwich while waiting for a cable car.
4. The first customer of the day always gets a discount—or so claims the Shopkeepers International Inc.
5. Wisdom comes in all shapes and sizes.
6. Express passes can always be as useful as a miracle man.
7. People with telepathic abilities are sometimes betrayed by bad travel advice or by a creature with a grudge.

Day 5

Singapore to Kuala Lumpur

We started our day early. The bus from Singapore to Kuala Lumpur was scheduled at 7.30 in the morning; however, the driver insisted that we be ready at 6 as it might take time to complete the formalities. We were dropped at the travel agency's office at 6.30, which was almost empty. There was just one woman taking care of all the formalities, which, it turned out, were not many. All she wanted to see was our bus tickets. Dad tried to show her our visas, but she interrupted. She told us that immigration and other formalities had to be done only on the border, and then asked us to wait for another cab which was supposed to take us to the bus. We had to wait for almost forty-five minutes before the cab arrived and took us to East Coast Road, where the bus to Kuala Lumpur was waiting.

The bus seemed to be very comfortable, with facilities like reclining seats, attached earphones, and Wi-Fi. The moment we got in, the attendant gave each of us a water bottle and a pack of biscuits. Wow, I thought. It was going to be a great road trip. Actually, it was me who suggested there should be a long road trip in our itinerary, and if anything went wrong, I knew, only I would be blamed. Thankfully, it was all looking comfortable—at least for now. As soon as the bus started to move, I dozed off.

I got up after the bus halted with a sudden jerk. I was trying to come back to my senses, when I heard the bus attendant saying that we've reached the immigration checkpoint. Oh yes, I completely forgot, it was an international border crossing. Of course, we'll have to go through the boring process of immigration.

All the passengers got off the bus for exit passport checks and then returned to the bus to cross the bridge to the Malaysian side. Very quick, I thought, but the real problem was yet to come. At the Malaysian checkpoint, we had to unload all our luggage and get it scanned. The usual custom clearance took a bit longer than expected. Overall, the whole process took about an hour. I was constantly wondering whether the bus would wait for us this long or not. Of course it was supposed to wait, as it was the responsibility of the operators to drop us at KL.

When we reached the bus, I was relieved to see that it was still waiting. We put the luggage back in the bus and took our seats. Now, it was our turn to wait, as two of the passengers still hadn't come back from the custom. The bus driver waited for another fifteen minutes, and then after talking to someone on the phone, started the bus. One of our co-passengers asked the attendant about that. The attendant replied in a very calm manner, 'Sir, sometimes the immigration officials detain some passengers for further inquiries. And if someone is detained by immigration for whatever reason, we at the bus wouldn't be able to find out for how long they are going to be there. Then it would be unfair to the other passengers to continue waiting as they may have flights to catch or other appointments. That's why we cannot wait indefinitely.'

'But what will happen to those two passengers now?' I chipped in.

'Oh, you don't worry about them. They have their luggage with them. As soon as they are cleared by customs, they can take the next bus operated by our company using the same ticket.'

'And they know that they're supposed to take the next bus?'

'Yes, of course, the officials at the checkpoint will guide them.'

Thank God, I thought. This bus company is much more considerate than our main tour operators.

After the Malaysian customs, it took the bus about five hours to reach Berjaya Times Square, which is one of the many pick-up and drop-off points in Kuala Lumpur.

We were given the contact number of the driver who was going to be with us for the next few days. Dad called him, and he said that he was waiting for us at Berjaya Times Square itself. Wow, a great surprise! For a change, it was not us who had to wait. In five minutes, the driver appeared and introduced himself very warmly. His name was Nazrin and he was a local. I immediately liked the guy. We all like smiling people, don't we?

But then, I noticed—he came walking towards us and his taxi was nowhere in sight. I asked him if we were going to the hotel on foot.

'No, no, we are not.' He laughed. 'Although your hotel is at a walking distance from here—but with all this luggage, no, no.'

'Then where is your car?' I wanted to clear the doubt.

'Oh, it is in the parking. I will take your luggage. In the meantime, I want you all to take a round of the Times Square. It is huge and worth seeing.'

'But we don't know what to see there.'

'Then let us go to the parking, keep the luggage in the car, and I will guide you through, if you like.'

Dad gladly accepted his offer. I was sure, Dad too must have liked him then and there. Nazrin was not only very cheerful, he seemed very helpful as well.

Berjaya Times Square is big. Nazrin showed us the main areas and kept talking about the building. He told us that the building has forty-eight stories in one tower, and nineteen in the other. It has a large shopping mall with over one thousand retail shops. It also has a hotel with twelve hundred luxury service suites, business offices and leisure centre, sixty-five food outlets, and indoor entertainment attractions such as the Berjaya Times Square Amusement Park. Wow! This guy was actually a good guide.

On our way to the hotel, Nazrin told us about our itinerary for the next day. Today, as we had a free evening as per the schedule given by the tour operator, Nazrin's services weren't required. He dropped us at the hotel and promised to come the next morning. Now it was up to Dad to decide what to do next, as he was the chief planner of our trip.

'We are going to Manish's place in the evening. He'll come and pick us from the hotel,' Dad announced.

'I believe Manish is that friend of yours who you mentioned while planning the trip, isn't he?' I chipped in.

'Yes, Joy, the same guy. And I'm sure you will enjoy the evening at his place. He has two sons, slightly older than you.'

'Let us see, Dad. All I've been doing so far is enjoying the evenings because of the hassles created by the tour operator.'

'What?'

'No, I really mean it. The tour operator always forgets to do something and we've to do on the spot rectifications. And of course, I'm enjoying this crisis management on daily basis.'

'I don't know what to say. You're being sarcastic, aren't you?'

'Of course not, Dad. I'm learning a lot from these experiences. This is how one becomes street smart, isn't it?'

'I guess so. Now let's get some rest.'

We were resting in the hotel room when the phone rang. It was the receptionist saying that one Mr Oberoi was waiting for us in the lounge. Yes, I'll have the chance of meeting one more character today, I thought. We got ready and went downstairs to the lobby. And there I saw a slightly overweight middle-aged Indian-looking man sitting on the sofa. He was immaculately dressed in a grey suit and a black tie as if he was here for a business meeting.

The moment he saw us, he almost jumped from the sofa and hugged Dad very tightly. He seemed delighted to meet us; it was evident from his body language. I greeted him in an equally happy looking way.

'Good evening, Manish uncle. How are you?'

'Good evening *beta*, I'm very fine. I'm so glad you all came here. I've been inviting your Dad for so long, ha ha ha.'

'Dad has told us so many things about you.'

'Oh, has he? Ha ha ha ha. Your Dad was one of the brightest students in our school. I was four years senior to your Dad and—most importantly—not so good at studies. A backbencher, ha ha ha. And still, we were the best of buddies, ha ha ha.'

Fake personality alert, my brain gave signals. Four sentences and four loud ha ha-type laughs. But I decided to give him some more time before jumping to any conclusion and kept this alert to myself. I noticed that Dad was still trapped in the tight grip of Mr Oberoi.

'How have you been, Manish?' Dad asked, trying to free himself from Mr Oberoi's strong arms.

'Oh, I'm very fine. Your brother is doing pretty well here in Kuala Lumpur, practically running half the city, ha ha ha ha.'

'Oh wow! And who's running the other half?'

Dad sounded sarcastic. But to me only, it seemed, as Mr Oberoi still kept laughing, and replied very simply.

'Oh, not sure about the other half. And I don't care who else is doing what. I'm happy with what I'm doing, ha ha ha ha.' Then he set Dad free from his clasp, as if doing a favour.

'Nice suit you're wearing.' Dad tried to give a compliment.

'Oh, thank you. This is a Brioni Vanquish II. Set me back about two hundred thousand ringgits. That would be about thirty-five lakh INR.'

'Yes brother, you always deserved that.'

Again, I sensed some sarcasm in Dad's voice. But it didn't bother Mr Oberoi. He was so engrossed in his hearty laughs. But again, who announces the price of his attire under three minutes of meeting someone? *This friend of Dad is certainly an interesting character*—I thought. Isn't he behaving like 'Mr Price Tag' from *3 Idiots*? Or is he a much bigger Price Tag himself.

'Let's go home then, ha ha ha ha,' Mr Oberoi announced happily. Then he guided us to the porch of the hotel, where his car was parked. I wondered how much the car cost. In fact, it was looking really expensive.

'This is my new Mercedes-Benz Maybach. Although we have a fleet of cars for the family, I decided that I'll bring this here, ha ha ha ha.' Mr Oberoi possibly read my mind and announced in a loud voice.

'Oh dear, this is a beauty. How much did this set you

back?' Dad said in a plain tone. It was difficult to tell whether he was being sarcastic again or he genuinely wanted to know the price.

'1.8 million ringgits. You know what, I got a good deal. Just after I brought this home, the prices went up.'

'Manish, bro, you were always very smart. See, Joy, one has to be this successful in life. Your Manish uncle is an inspiration.'

Here, I really wanted Dad to stop being so sarcastic. Mr Oberoi could sense it anytime now. But it looked like Dad was enjoying himself. After all, Mr Oberoi was behaving exactly like Dad predicted yesterday. And the funny part was that Mr Oberoi too was enjoying himself.

Mr Oberoi drove us to his home through the beautiful and lively streets of Kuala Lumpur. I enjoyed the drive despite the usual evening traffic. We reached his home in 20 to 25 minutes, which was located in Bangsar. It was a large and beautiful bungalow. I was impressed by its sheer size and grandeur, even though Mr Oberoi had not yet announced its price. However, Dad was hell bent on provoking him to show off again.

'Nice bungalow you have, Manish, and what a posh locality. It seems all the rich people live here.'

'Oh, thanks, buddy. As a matter of fact, Bangsar is home to many of Kuala Lumpur's elites and expatriates. From here to the park, this enclave has several lavish and sophisticated bungalows and villas. I bought this house six years back, ha ha ha ha.'

Thank God, he didn't mention the price of the house. We were spared with only a simple—ha ha. How humble of him. I noticed one more thing. Mr Oberoi was very loud and fast when he talked. Sentences came out of his mouth very quickly as if he wanted to spill out as many words as possible in one go. Interesting, I thought.

As we entered the palatial house of Mr Oberoi, we were greeted at the door by Mrs Oberoi. She had a warm smile on her face. My mind started trying to figure out whether this smile was real or not. Then, suddenly, I scolded myself for this. There's no way you can go on judging every person you see—not done. I freed my mind from this useless exercise and greeted Mrs Oberoi.

Mrs Oberoi smiled again and greeted me by patting my back. Mr Oberoi then led us to a large and ornate living room. Wow! This family definitely has good taste. Then Mr Oberoi introduced me to his sons, Mihir and Mahip. Mihir came forward and said in a loud voice, 'Come, Joy, I will show you around.' As a matter of fact, I really wanted to see their big house, so I willingly accompanied him.

Mihir first took me to his room and started showing me the furniture and other accessories, not forgetting to tell me the prices of everything. Just like his father, Mihir also seemed to be more interested in the price of a commodity rather than its utility. Like father, like son! I thought, when Mahip chipped in. He wanted to show me his new PS-5, which his father gave him as a Sunday gift last week.

'A Sunday gift?'

'Yeah bro, Pa takes us out on Sundays and allows us to buy anything of our choice.'

'You mean both of you buy something on Sundays?'

'Generally, yes.'

'And you may choose anything?'

'Oh, not very expensive things. Around RM 3000–4000.'

I was speechless. Impressed too. RM 4000—dope, man. I didn't know how to react. Thankfully, the boys weren't in a habit of firing ha ha ha like their '*pa*', otherwise I would have had the feeling that they were laughing at me. Deep pockets.

We played some games on his PS-5. Thankfully, the two super-rich brothers were quiet during the game, and I had the opportunity of coming back to my senses. However, I was pretty sure that my dear Dad would still be facing the bombardment of ha ha ha in some other room of this huge palace—poor him.

Then Mrs Oberoi came to the room. She gently asked us to join the elders for dinner. She seemed different from the males of the family, I thought.

We went to the dining room. Mr Oberoi was sitting next to Dad, and they were talking about their school days. I was happy to see that Dad was an active participant in the discussion. Moreover, when he spoke, Mr Oberoi listened. Wow! This man does listen sometimes. Although he didn't seem comfortable with someone else speaking and kept smirking at Dad frequently. Yet he was listening. And that made my mood lift again.

Dinner was wonderful. The table was full of vegetarian delights from all over the world. Mr Oberoi had tried his best to be a good host. I don't want to take anything away from him. He was genuinely happy to meet us. The showing-off part was there, of course, but it seemed to be part of his personality—he simply couldn't help it. Mrs Oberoi was without doubt a very graceful host. Overall, the whole family was nice, and they made sure we enjoyed at their place.

Lessons Learnt

1. Not all pickup drivers are poker-faced. Sometimes, if you're lucky, you may come across the happy-go-lucky kind.
2. Some people suffer mental trauma when they have nothing to show off.
3. Don't judge a person too quickly. Judge the person slowly, and you may arrive at the exact same result.
4. It is okay to quote the price of an item at an auction, but definitely not required at a social gathering.

Day 6

Kuala Lumpur

My day began with a hangover—courtesy of an overdose of the great Oberoi show-off. I needed some time to recover from that by staying in bed for an extended period—but that was not to be. As per the travellers' protocol, orally drafted by dear Dad, I was forced to get ready *as quickly as possible.*

Today, we were heading to the famous Batu Caves, followed by a city tour and, finally, a visit to the iconic Petronas Twin Towers. Dad and Mumma were ready, and I was expected to join them for breakfast in 20 minutes.

I succumbed to the situation and, with my best efforts, managed to get ready in 19 minutes and 47 seconds. God! Why was I turning more and more like Dad!

We grabbed a quick breakfast and headed to the hotel lobby, where our driver Nazrin was waiting. He had a new car again today. I couldn't stop wondering if the car agency was also inspired by Mr Oberoi—a brand-new car every day!

Nazrin, a veritable fountain of local lore and trivia, drove us to Batu Caves. As we approached, the awe-inspiring limestone marvel loomed over us, its grandeur whispering tales of ancient magnificence. Batu Caves feature several grand structures. The main temple is situated inside the cave, with 272 steps leading up to it.

We entered the premises and, immediately, Mumma was drawn to colourful shops near the gate. The shops were selling everything from glittering ornaments to rainbow-coloured garments, tiny wooden elephants, and more refrigerator magnets than any family could ever need in a lifetime. We hadn't even entered the caves yet, and Mumma was already negotiating with a vendor about some beaded necklace that would look just *lovely* on her.

Dad, who was apparently still in *Temple Visit Mode*, sighed and glanced up at the towering 272 steps, which, to be honest, looked like they were about to test the limits of human endurance.

'Hey,' he said, 'let's do the temple visit first. The shopping project can wait, I guess. See, the caves are calling us.'

'Fine!' she said, reluctantly putting the beads down—but not before giving them one last longing look.

'But what if someone else buys it before we come back?' she asked Dad.

'No one is going to buy that, rest assured. Besides, there are several sellers here, and all of them must be having similar items,' Dad replied.

Meanwhile, Mumma, after leaving the bead shop, suddenly spotted a vendor selling scarves.

'Wait! Look at this! It'll look so beautiful on you!' she exclaimed, grabbing Dad's arm as though it were the last lifeline on a sinking ship. But Dad was mentally prepared for the climb.

'Later,' he said.

'But it's only 20 ringgits!' She protested.

'Later, dear.' Dad was unmoved.

After a few more rounds of discussions about souvenirs, garments, and decorative items that could *wait*—according to Dad—we finally started our ascent. And, man, those steps to the caves were something! Not just steps—they looked like a fitness test. But to Dad, they seemed like a cakewalk. He powered through them as if running a race. For sure, he wanted to be as far from the shops as possible. Mumma was careful while climbing—taking one step at a time.

And me? I was basically at the front, pretending to be a part of some superhero squad on a mission to save the world from… well, more beads, shawls, and souvenirs.

My mission was hilariously interrupted by the arrival of a broad-shouldered man. He suddenly stepped in front of us and smiled.

'Hi guys!'

'Hi there!' I spoke.

'These steps are an obstacle course, right?' He smiled again.

'No, not that much. We've just started,' I replied.

'Good! My name is Magne, and I'm from Norway.'

'I'm Joy and these are my parents. We're from India.'

'Oh great! First time here?' He decided to talk to Dad now.

'Yes, Magne. And you?' Dad inquired.

'No, no, definitely not the first time. Nor second or third. I feel a special connection to this place. Whenever I get a chance, I come here,' Magne replied.

'From Norway?' Dad asked again.

'Well, not exactly. I am a Norwegian alright, but I work in Kuala Lumpur. I am a press correspondent.'

'I get it.' It was Dad's turn to smile.

'That is why I come here almost every weekend,' Magne said.

'You must be well versed with the history of this place then. Is it true that these limestone caves are ancient?'

'Yes, brother, these caves are really old. This place was once occupied by the indigenous tribes of Temuan people, and later the Chinese community harvested the place for fertilizing residues. The idea of converting this place to a Shrine was given by one Mr Pillai. He established the large golden statue of Lord Murugan at the entrance of the temple.'

Man, this guy had a wealth of knowledge about this place. Dad and Mumma definitely seemed impressed. Magne climbed the steps with us, and with the enthusiasm of a caffeinated historian and the confidence of a man with Wi-Fi in his brain, regaled us with the history of the temple, the caves, and the places in Kuala Lumpur worth visiting. He managed to recount it in a manner that was both entertaining and informative—peppered with dramatic flourishes and theatrical hand gestures.

'Magne, what about these tiring steps? Were they always this colourful?' I asked.

'Joy, previously, these steps were wooden. The wood was swapped with concrete in 1920. What's more, these steps are not exactly tiring. If you keep taking short breaks, take selfies, and talk to people, preferably in their language, you will enjoy the climb.'

'You speak the local language?'

'Of course, I do,' Magne said and tried engaging locals in Bahasa, or at least what he claimed was Bahasa. The locals nodded and smiled, probably wondering why this tall Norwegian was speaking a language that was almost, but not quite, entirely unlike Malay.

Following Magne's instructions, we took several selfie breaks, enjoyed the scenery, and listened carefully to more instructions by Magne. Noticing our interest, or perhaps just seizing an audience, Magne silently declared himself our guide. We—swept up in his boundless energy and dubious expertise—accepted his hidden proclamation. Owing to our guide's captivating monologue, we didn't even realize when all the steps were climbed and when we had reached the top!

There were many temples inside the cave, and the area was spacious enough to accommodate a few hundred of them. A row of peacock sculptures lined the railing in front of the temple. We explored every temple and shrine within—each more magnificent than the last. Magne accompanied us to all the temples and narrated the stories behind them. We were genuinely grateful to him, as his presence greatly helped us understand the historical and cultural significance of Batu Caves.

However, the one thing Magne's encyclopaedic knowledge failed to cover was the location of the toilets. In fact, there weren't any inside the cave. We had to wait till we came out of the cave complex to find one.

After our cave odyssey, filled to the brim with facts and an inexplicable but profound appreciation for indoor plumbing, we emerged into the sunlight. Apparently, the challenge now was to find a toilet first. And it wasn't Magne who won the quest—Dad found one.

Then we sat inside a restaurant. Magne—still brimming with facts and enthusiasm—joined us for snacks. Between bites of idlis and samosas, we exchanged stories and laughter. I had a feeling of contentment—finally able to rest my legs after that gruelling StairMaster session. We had a great day so far. The caves were wonderful, the climb was long but enjoyable, and Magne's company was delightful. And not to forget the idlis at the Tamil restaurant in the cave premises—delicious.

However, there was still one thing missing—Phase-2 of the mission Batu Caves: shopping. Without doubt, the *later* Dad was referring to was *now*. Mumma purchased all the small things she wanted—for herself, me, Dad, our friends, our relatives, and of course, Magne. When Mumma handed Magne his gift, he was overwhelmed, 'Oh dear, thank you so much, but I think, I should buy you guys something—for your wonderful company.'

'Magne, thank you for being our guide and showing us around. It helps when someone in the group knows the place,' Mumma said graciously.

'But if you allow me, I want to say something about the souvenirs you have picked up,' Magne replied

'Yeah sure, go ahead,' said Mumma.

'Don't you think you have overpaid for these items? You could have purchased the same things from the Bukit Bintang Street Market at much lower prices.'

'You didn't get the point, Magne. It's not about the prices—it's about memories. We'll quickly remember the place every time we see these little things.' Mumma was spot on.

Not only Magne, but I too was speechless. Yes—now I could see the point. This is the reason why Mumma is always eager to buy overpriced items from tourist spots.

Our next destination today was the iconic Petronas Twin Towers, a gleaming testament to the modern marvel that is Malaysia—and the setting for millions of selfies every day. As we reached closer, the towers looked like beacons of progress and the ultimate homage to the spirit of *I'm taller than you.*

Our entry tickets included the services of a guide as well. We had hardly entered the premises when we heard a shrieking voice—which, of course, belonged to our guide.

'Group number 7, please gather here!' she almost screamed, as if testing our decibel-bearing capacity. Dad nearly jumped, Mumma clutched her bag a little too tightly, and I couldn't help noticing how quickly our group members assembled. Here, we were herded into a group of fifteen travellers from different parts of the globe.

As we stood at the entrance, our guide embarked on a comprehensive exposition of the tower's history, architecture, and significance—like a robot on low battery. Clearly, she had been doing this job for longer than I had been alive, and it looked like she was ready to sell her soul to the first person who offered her a nap—that too on prices significantly lower than what one pays at Bukit Bintang Street Market for *souvenirs*.

I could tell that she had already given this lecture about six to seven times since the morning. Her words were like a well-rehearsed monologue. 'The towers were built in 1998. They are 452 metres tall, etc, etc.' She continued with the enthusiasm of someone reading the instructions on a gadget box.

No tour group is ever complete without a Mr or Miss Curiosity. Our group was no exception. We had an old Australian guy with us, who apparently had some knowledge of basic masonry.

'Wat kind of material 'as been used fawr the found-aye-tions?' he asked.

The guide answered like she was reading from a manual, 'High strength concrete, sir.'

'What about the windows, then? Aah they ma-ye-d of bulletproof glass?' Mr Curiosity wasn't deterred.

'Yes, sir. High-quality bulletproof glass.'

'So, if oi threw a rock at it, would it break?'

I could see the poor, tired guide mentally calculating how many more hours she'll have to work today, handling tourists like the beloved Australian. She gave up and said calmly, 'Sir, please don't throw rocks at the windows. I'll lose my job, your group won't be able to finish the tour, and you yourself might end up in prison.'

The answer had a positive impact. Mr Curiosity didn't ask any further questions for next three minutes. However, he couldn't hold himself for long, and restarted his civil engineering-related questions soon. However, the questions coming in now were more carefully structured, and the guide—while answering them—could slip back into her 'pre-recorded announcement' mode. I couldn't help but miss dear Magne. As a guide, Magne—with his larger-than-life personality and endless stream of trivia—would have turned this tour into a theatrical production, complete with dramatic pauses, and perhaps a re-enactment of the towers' construction. He would probably have had us performing mock interviews with imaginary engineers. But then, who knows what would have been his own reaction, if he had to deal with aged masons from Sydney 10 times a day!

I, personally benefitted a lot from the flurry of questions by the big old Aussie, and it was like I had got a backstage pass to Petronas Twin Towers' builders' and managers' office. When the Aussie realized I was listening intently to his questions, he began sharing countless tips on building processes. By the end of the tour, I was thoroughly acquainted with every type of concrete ever used in Malaysia and Australia, and felt fully prepared to write a dissertation on tower architecture.

Inside the towers, we were shuffled along like well-dressed cattle, pausing briefly at points of interest where our guide would point out architectural features and historical titbits with the enthusiasm of a young mother of twins—who soil their nappies every 10 minutes.

'And here, we have the Skybridge, which connects the two towers and offers a stunning view of the city.'

Fascinating stuff—though it would have been even more thrilling had we been allowed to dwell on it for more than thirty seconds before being herded to the next highlight. Literally, we passed more times inside the elevators than on the floors. The observation deck was on the eighty-sixth floor, and thankfully, our kind guide allowed us sufficient time to enjoy the panoramic views of Kuala Lumpur.

Finally, we finished the tour, and I glanced back at our guide. Her smile was as strained as a rubber band stretched too tight. She seemed even more exhausted than when we started, yet had to be ready for another group of eccentric travellers to test her patience.

'Group 8, follow me!' she announced. Her voice echoed through the hall, as if she was bracing herself for another round of questions like 'What colour is the Skybridge on a cloudy day?'

Nazrin was waiting for us in the parking area. It was great to see a smiling face again after a long time. And he had a surprise for us.

'You know, sir, I know a great South Indian restaurant in Bukit Bintang area where you are staying. I'll drop you there after we take a round of the city,' he said in a typical, happy tone.

'Oh Nazrin, thank you so much. I forgot to do the research myself. Which restaurant is that?' Dad asked.

'Sir, it's Saravana Bhavan.'

'Oh, they have a branch almost everywhere in the world. But why a South Indian one?'

'Sir, I know your fascination for South Indian cuisine. My company told me that.'

'Very well, Nazrin. You drop us there and we'll walk to the hotel after dinner.'

'No issues, sir, I'll collect you from there. Walking to your hotel from Saravana Bhavan may be tiresome. It's Christmas tomorrow, and I don't want you to be too tired to wake up late in the morning.'

'Well, we want to have a look at the street market in Bukit Bintang. We have heard a lot about its price competitiveness.' Dad looked at Mumma and they both laughed.

'Sure, sir.'

Nazrin definitely knew how to do his job perfectly. And me? I definitely knew—it was going to be another rasam-rice night for me. That too on Christmas eve—poor me!

Lessons Learnt

1. Give greater regard to Scandinavian wisdom than to Oriental wisdom, especially when you encounter Norwegian dudes the size of The Rock, with a thirst for historical knowledge.
2. It's not always about the price—it's about the memories you make.
3. Concrete is a composite construction material composed of cement, water, and aggregates as its main constituents. The three main types of concrete are normal-strength concrete, reinforced concrete, and plain concrete. *Courtesy: Mr Curiosity.*
4. Cut your tour guides some slack. They may be tormented by the baffling questions of a civil engineering aficionado.

Day 7

Kuala Lumpur

Yesterday was exhausting. First, the endurance-testing 272 steps of Batu Caves, then the hassles at the Petronas Twin Towers, and finally the long walk back from Saravana Bhavan to the hotel. Thankfully, today we were scheduled to visit Sunway Lagoon—Kuala Lumpur's very own jungle of thrill rides, a variety of water slides, and entertainment shows.

It was Christmas morning, and I had already come to terms with the fact that this year Santa would not be dropping by my house. And apparently, he doesn't make stops in hotels with fancy breakfast spreads.

I was feeling a bit gloomy about the whole thing. Guided by my parents, I walked into the restaurant for breakfast, hoping to at least get a croissant to drown my disappointment in carbs.

And then—I saw a girl I thought I knew. Well, what are the chances, I murmured to myself. Was she a random girl that looked like her? No, no—it was really her!

'Kriti!'

'Oh hello, Joy! What on earth are you doing here?' She jumped with excitement.

Kriti was my classmate. I could also see her seven-year-old brother, Daksh, sipping on a glass of orange juice. Wow! What a coincidence! These are the same people who I would normally see fighting over the last slice of pizza in a cafeteria back in Dehradun!

'I have the same question for you. When did you come to Kuala Lumpur?' I asked.

'We arrived last night. You?' Kriti asked.

'We came here the day before yesterday,' I replied.

'From India?' asked Kriti again.

'No, we were in Singapore before this,' I said.

'How long are you staying here?' asked Kriti again.

'Tomorrow we are taking a flight to Thailand. This is our last day here,' I replied.

'Oh, we'll be here for next two days, then we'll go to Singapore,' Kriti said.

'Thankfully, it's Christmas, and we can celebrate it together,' I said.

Now, there's a rule about school friends. When you see them outside of school, it's like a superpower is unlocked. You forget about everything else in the world, like your parents, breakfast, and the fact that your cab is waiting in the hotel porch to take you to Sunway Lagoon in 20 minutes. You just want to have fun with them—immediately.

However, since we were running short of time, we quickly joined them on the breakfast table. Mumma and Dad already knew Kriti's parents, so thankfully, I didn't have to go through the cumbersome process of introducing them to each other.

'Joy, how are you planning to celebrate Christmas?' Kriti's dad asked.

'We are going to an amusement park. In fact, our cab is waiting,' I replied.

'Our cab is waiting as well. We are going to Sunway Lagoon,' Kriti chirped in.

'What? Are you serious?'

'What?'

'Sunway Lagoon? Actually, we are also going there.' I was really excited now. They were here for Sunway Lagoon! I mean, can it get any better than that? It was Christmas, and instead of lounging at home watching some random Christmas movie—most likely *Home Alone 2*, definitely a repeat from last year—we were going to Sunway Lagoon! That too, together!

After grabbing a quick breakfast, we came out to the porch. We were hardly surprised when it turned out that we would be sharing the same cab. Same tour operators, I guessed. We chose our seats as expected. Parents together and kids together. Kriti's brother Daksh was very excited, and their father had to stop him several times while he tried bouncing off the walls of the cab, basically an embodiment of the thrill ride we were heading towards.

As we reached the gates of the enormous amusement park, me and my family walked up to the ticket counter—all smiles and ready to go. Apparently, either our entry tickets were well stamped, or someone from the Singapore operators' team had already sent the message to these guys to be extra careful while handling Dad. In fact, the guys at the entry gate greeted us like we were regulars. I'll be honest—we barely had to show the stamped tickets. They didn't even ask for our IDs. No one dared question the 'Dad discount'. I could literally see the tour guide nodding in respectful acknowledgement of Dad's *previous adventures with complicated tickets*, and probably some other situation where Dad had probably *fixed* a problem using nothing but his calm demeanour and the precise ability to talk to any agency like a pro.

Kriti's family, however, didn't seem to have the same privilege. Her dad certainly lacked my dad's charisma. They were stopped at the counter and the entry gate guys took forever to check their coupons.

As it turned out, their coupons hadn't been properly stamped. The guard looked at the pile of papers produced by Kriti's dad, then at the faces of the family, and then back at the papers—as if they were a cryptic treasure map that only an expert could decipher.

Kriti's mom, trying to remain calm, said, 'Are you sure we have the right ones? They all look the same.'

Her dad again pulled out another stack of papers. There was a small mountain of coupons, each one more confusing than the other. He was sweating bullets, flipping through them as if he was suddenly auditioning for the role of Tom Cruise's sidekick in the next instalment of *Mission Impossible.*

And just as panic started to settle in and I imagined our entire group was going to be trapped at the gate for the next few hours, Dad swooped in. He walked over with his classic 'Let me handle this' swagger, took one look at the coupon mess, then looked straight into the eyes of the guard, and said in an extremely composed voice, 'They are with us.'

Neither could I explain it, nor Kriti and her family. In three seconds—I swear in three seconds—the expressions on the guard's face changed. He blinked, then smiled, then selected the right coupons himself, and in an instant, Kriti's family was in: no fuss, no argument. Just the sound of a tiny paper being exchanged and *boom*, the gates opened. They didn't even check the rest of the tickets.

Kriti and I exchanged wide-eyed looks. Kriti's parents, however, were in shock. They still couldn't believe their eyes. Dad had just turned a coupon crisis into a smooth victory.

They must have been convinced that Dad had some secret identity as a professional coupon negotiator.

Sunway Lagoon is a big amusement park with over ninety attractions. It also has an interactive zoo housing over one hundred and forty species. Today, it was looking even more attractive owing to Christmas. It was like Santa had taken a detour and decided to set up the North Pole right in the heart of Kuala Lumpur. The place was decked out in oversized candy canes, big hoardings, and enough tinsel to make you question if they had raided an entire warehouse of holiday decorations.

It was impossible to cover the whole of it in a day, so we decided to prioritize our activities. We selected the Scream Park as our first destination. But of course, it was Mumma's idea. She was already eyeing the haunted house with the kind of intensity that only comes from watching one too many 'Based on a True Story' ghost documentaries on YouTube late at night.

The show was good—but scary. At first, it was all fun. We laughed, chatted about the creepy paintings on the walls, and made jokes about how, if a ghost appeared, we'd totally outsmart it by slapping it across the face.

But as we moved forward, it was clear to me that this show wasn't just scary—it was intentionally designed to mess with our minds. Every time you turned a corner, you were expecting something to jump out—but it never did. It was the unnerving tension that was the real terror here.

Then, one by one, we visited the World of Adventures, Surf Beach, Wild West, and Waters of Africa. As sunset neared, and after enjoying most of the rides and water slides, we decided to eat something at one of the many restaurants inside the park.

It was here when Kriti's brother, Daksh, decided to come into the picture as a wild card entrant. Yes, Daksh, the 7-year-old tornado who had been happily soaking in the water slides and rides. But just like the best kind of Christmas drama, it only took one thing to flip the script—the feeling of being ignored.

You see, Daksh had been doing what he did best: playing, laughing, and causing general mayhem. But suddenly, as we were heading to the restaurant to refuel after all those slides, it hit him—an unsettling realization. He wasn't the centre of attention. And what better time to change that than when a group of Christmas-clad performers was singing carols and spreading Christmas cheer? I mean, if you're going to make a scene, it might as well be a Christmas one.

As we walked towards the performance, the carollers were in full swing, their voices blending with the jingle bells. You could almost hear the 'Ho-ho-ho' vibes in the air.

But Daksh had other ideas. Without hesitation, he darted forward like a small, over-caffeinated elf on a mission, and tried to 'commandeer the microphone'. And let me tell you—these performers were saints, truly. They handed him the mic, probably hoping he would just belt out a few lyrics and we could all move on with our Christmas lunch.

But Daksh wasn't done. Oh no, no, no! With the mic now in his tiny, triumphant hands, he sang a barely-recognizable 'Jingle Bells' at a decibel level that could easily rival a fire truck siren. The performers nodded and smiled through the whole thing, keeping their Christmas cheer intact. Clearly, they were trying to stay in the holiday spirit.

Of course, until the next phase of Daksh's grand plan began.

In a move that can only be described as **bold**, Daksh

suddenly decided the drummer needed to hand over his sticks. And by 'needed', I mean Daksh 'demanded' them. Now, I'm not sure if it was the drumsticks or the thrill of public disruption, but Daksh wasn't leaving without them. The drummer, understandably, was reluctant to part with them. Things were going out of hands—quite literally. But the show must go on, right? Daksh wasn't deterred. He grabbed, pulled, and tugged with the energy of a thousand Christmas lights tangled in a box.

As expected, the drummer held on, and Daksh—realizing his power wasn't limitless—pulled out the ace from his bag of pandemonium-causing tricks—he started crying. Now, the whole audience was watching—their absolute attention on Daksh and his escalating 'performances'. His parents looked like they were trying to negotiate peace in a hostage situation. His mom was doing her absolute best to talk him down, but Daksh had entered full tantrum mode. Even I used to be a seven-year-old sometimes back, but this 'mayhem' was out of my comprehension.

The staff members, still trying to maintain their festive composure, tried to calm Daksh—but he was on a roll. I mean, what's Christmas without a bit of theatrical chaos, right? He wasn't just making noise—he was making a statement. The kid had an 'audience' finally, and he wasn't about to let it go to waste.

I looked at Dad, hoping for some timely intervention; however, he was watching the spectacle like it was the most interesting thing that had happened all day. In fact, he looked positively uninterested in engaging. He had that 'I'm a spectator, not a participant' vibe. Thanks, Dad, for your nonchalance.

That's when Kriti and I knew it was time for us to take

charge of the situation. We exchanged a glance. This wasn't our first rodeo. We had dealt with cafeteria tantrums in school before, and we knew how to manage a spoilt brat with an audience. So, we launched into action.

Kriti started with the subtle distraction. 'Hey Daksh, do you want to see the giant Christmas tree outside? It's got lights and everything!'

'No. I want to play the drums.' Daksh, being Daksh, wasn't taking the bait.

Finally, I had to pull out the big guns.

'Wait, did you hear? I got a call from the guys at our hotel. They are distributing Christmas special drums with sticks to those who play drums well. But I don't think you're going to get them.'

'Why not?'

'Because you're just an average drum player. Be happy with these sticks.'

'No, I'm a good drummer. I don't want these. Let's go to the hotel—now!'

'Let us eat something first. They don't give Christmas gifts to hungry kids.'

And just like that, Daksh's eyes lit up. Who needs these local, unattractive drumsticks when there are special, decorated ones on the line? His tantrum fizzled out like a forgotten Christmas candle, and with all the drama suddenly behind us, he skipped away happily, hand-in-hand with Kriti.

His parents were looking at me in disbelief. They were possibly thinking that everyone in my family has a degree in overcoming difficult situations. Kriti came nearer. She whispered in my ears, 'Joy, Daksh is again going to create a scene at the hotel when he finds out there is no such offer.'

'Who said there's no offer?'

'What do you mean?'

'Ask your dad to stop at Bukit Bintang Street Market when we go back. He can buy a well decorated toy-drum from there. I'm very sure he'll get anything from there at *competitive prices*.' I winked.

Mumma got the joke and smiled at me. And Dad? He, who had been quietly supervising the whole incident like some kind of Christmas-sheriff! He was no longer nonchalant. His eyes were full of admiration for me. He had evidence now that his superpower of handling situations has smoothly been passed on to his offspring. After all, genes work.

While coming back to the hotel, Kriti sat with me. I could see in her eyes that she was still thankful for officially saving Christmas.

'Joy, you're going tomorrow?' she said.

'Yeah, that's what the itinerary says.'

'It was great to have you with us today. We still have five to six days of our trip left. How will we manage Daksh without you?'

'That's what a trip is all about. Learn and survive.' I chuckled.

Lessons Learnt

1. Theme-park enthusiasts should be trained by tour operators in the subtle art of handling tickets.
2. A well-told, silly little lie, and a touch of charisma, is all it takes to outwit a nefarious attention seeker.
3. With its competitive prices, Bukit Bintang Street might just overtake Wall Street in terms of financial transactions. *Courtesy: Spendthrift Moms.*

Day 8

Kuala Lumpur to Bangkok and Pattaya

The flight from Kuala Lumpur to Bangkok was 'nothing to write home about' type. As the tour operator booked us on a so-called low-cost airline, several things were missing. Water was given just once and it wasn't free. Subsequently, the seatback monitors of the in-flight entertainment system weren't working—and where they did, earphones weren't provided. Mumma asked the crew and was told that we had to rent the earphones for 10 ringgits. I was left with the option to watch the clouds from the window. Dad gave me a smile, as if saying what else could be expected from an 'economical' airline. However, the pilot must have been very skilled, as it was a smooth flight—we didn't feel any turbulence.

We reached the Don Mueang International Airport in Bangkok around 11 in the morning. Kuala Lumpur to Bangkok was not exactly a long flight, but still, we all were feeling famished. After completing visa and immigration procedures and purchasing local SIMs, we went to the nearest Starbucks and ordered some pancakes.

Our welcome in Bangkok was quite interesting. A guide from the tour operator's local unit greeted us at the exit gate.

She was holding a large placard, which showed not only our names but our pictures as well. She matched our faces to the pictures on the placard, quickly took one more family picture, sent it to her bosses, and after confirmation—which she got within seconds—escorted us towards the parking area.

As per the itinerary, we were headed straight to Pattaya, where we were staying for three nights. The cab that came to pick us up, first took us to Suvarnabhumi Airport, where another cab was waiting for us to take us to Pattaya. The view on the way from Bangkok to Pattaya was breathtaking. The small hamlets and villages on route were scenic.

Pattaya is the glittering jewel of Thailand, where the neon lights never sleep and the fun—for single tourists and families—never ends. Our hotel was near the beach. It was a charming, spacious place with a suspiciously grand name that promised 'Luxury and Serenity.' We, somehow, discovered later that night that what it actually delivered was more along the lines of 'Luxury-ish and the Sound of Karaoke till 3 a.m.'

Our tour Manager, Priaw, was waiting for us in the hotel lobby. She looked quite young—a whirlwind of efficiency and smiles. She handed us our tickets and briefed us about the itinerary we were to follow. First on her list was the Alcazar Cabaret Show. As she mentioned, it was a dance show. Mumma narrowed her eyes on the word 'cabaret'.

'Is the show okay for kids?' she asked, her voice tinged with maternal suspicion. Clearly, I wasn't adult enough to attend such things!

'Oh, nothing to worry about. Alcazar Cabaret Show is one of the city's most famous performances—suitable for both kids and adults. It's more Broadway glitz than back-alley blitz. Dance and theatre lovers won't want to miss this show. And the best part is that you have dance performances on Indian songs too.' Priaw chuckled warmly with the practiced patience of someone who has fielded this question a thousand times.

And she was not done. With a mischievous glint in her eyes, she added, 'For adults, Pattaya has many things to offer. But don't worry—we don't give those away as freebies! She winked, leaving us to wonder how many grown-up escapades she had seen in her tour-managing career.

Reassured, but intrigued, we headed to our room to freshen up—Mumma still murmuring about the appropriateness of this all. The room was actually a luxurious suite—spacious, beautifully decorated, and with a wonderful beach view from the balcony.

Suddenly, I had an urge to head to the beach. I was completely in a mood of becoming a pro at building sandcastles and maybe get a little tan—even though, let's be honest, getting a tan is not exactly ideal for Indians.

Mumma spotted something interesting. No, it wasn't the beach, it wasn't the big swimming pool and it wasn't the fact that there were souvenir shops on practically every corner of the hotel. It was, actually, the room service menu. Mumma had this moment where she turned into a detective, squinting at the menu card like she was trying to read ancient scrolls.

'Vegetarian Indian Thali,' she exclaimed, like she had just found the holy grail. Her eyes lit up like she had just discovered a treasure inside the hotel mini-fridge. 'Joy, you know what this means, right? No more sweating over finding an Indian restaurant. We've hit the jackpot.'

I looked at my Casio Pro Trek—it was 2.15. Yes, building sandcastles can wait till post lunch, I decided. We ordered the thali, and when it arrived, it was both surprising and delightful. I mean, the aroma hit us first—a wave of spices that immediately had me salivating. Dad's face broke into this goofy grin, 'It's just like home!' he said, diving in with enthusiasm. Honestly, it really tasted as good as the food back in India—the naans had the right level of heat, the dal makhani boasted just the right amount of spices, and the paneer in the curry was perfectly soft. We all dug in, and I was ready to declare with complete certainty that the chef in this hotel was from Punjab or Uttarakhand.

The Alcazar show was scheduled to begin at 7 p.m. That meant we still had some time to spare. After resting for a while, we decided to hit the beach. Christmas had just passed; however, the city was still in full celebration mode. The beach was packed—but surprisingly, most of the tourists were Indian. Not families, though. Nope! Maybe there were a few, but mostly *single Indian men*. And I don't mean single in the 'I'm just here for the sun' kind of way. Oh no—every single one of them seemed to be in a 'looking for a partner' mood, as if Pattaya was their personal matchmaking service.

And let me tell you, I don't think I had ever seen so many people pretending to casually glance at the ocean, while actually trying to figure out where the *scope* lies. The air was thick with energy. And here I was, trying to avoid getting sand inside my shoes.

Dad, of course, was totally oblivious to the beach's unofficial *Love Actually* re-enactment. He was too busy giving clichéd comments on how 'refreshing' the beach was and how 'nice' the waves looked. But Mumma was suspiciously aware of what was going on. 'You notice how there are so many Indian males here?' she raised an eyebrow. 'It's like a single's convention.'

'No, no, it's just the holiday crowd,' Dad said, totally missing the point, or perhaps pretending to.

Mumma just shook her head, and I tried to act like I didn't understand what this was all about.

Anyway, after a solid one hour of pretending not to notice all the spontaneous 'partner-finding tension' in the air, we decided to head back to the hotel. Mumma, however, ended up laughing about how totally different Pattaya was from what she had imagined. Well, Dad kept silent—he probably already knew what to expect from this shiny city.

Evening arrived and, tickets in hand, we made our way to the Alcazar Cabaret Show—an establishment that looked as though it had been bedazzled by a fairy godmother with a penchant for sequins.

The show started, and any lingering doubts Mumma had were quickly dispelled. The performers dazzled us with elaborate costumes, impeccable choreography, and a sense of flamboyant exuberance that could only be described as fabulous. There were dancers of every kind—Samba, Bollywood, K-pop, traditional Oriental, and more. Even the kids in the audience were mesmerized, eyes wide open as they took in the spectacle of lights and music.

Partway through the show, as a group of performers strutted onstage as Gypsy characters, Mumma leaned over and whispered, 'Priaw was right, I guess. It's just good, clean fun.' Just then, a performer did a high kick that revealed a bit more than Mumma's expectations. Mumma's eyes widened. 'Well, mostly clean,' she added with a cheeky smile.

As we exited the theatre after the show, we were all buzzing with excitement and humming the show tunes. Mumma, still slightly pink around the ears, admitted that the show had been a delightful surprise. I also felt the same. This was, by far, the most glamourous spectacle of lip-syncing, feather boas, and sparkles I had ever seen.

We decided to walk back to the hotel. Mumma pointed towards the side streets and said, 'These streets look so busy. They lead to the beach, right? Let's stroll through them.'

'These are called Sois. I don't think there's anything special there.' Dad seemed to be very cautious.

'There's no harm in seeing them.' Mumma insisted.

'Alright, if you say so.' Dad was still looking reluctant.

So, we turned towards one of the 'Sois' of Pattaya. And let me tell you, the streets were very alive with action. And by action, I mean 'Single Indian Men'. Everywhere. Everywhere! It looked as though the crowd had been flown in from every corner of India, as if there had been a secret sale on international flights to Thailand.

Now, I finally understood what Priaw meant when she said 'Pattaya has many things to offer to adults.' Clearly, she didn't mean 'A'-rated movie tickets or outdoor games for grown-ups—no, no. She was talking about this—the flashy neon signs that promised 'Special Services' and 'late night entertainment'. Apparently, these weren't freebies in the sense of complimentary dinner coupons by the tour operators.

I kept my cool, of course, flashing a 'I'm-12-so-too-young-and-ignorant-for-this' smile that hid my inner curiosity. But honestly, I was starting to wonder if I had just stumbled into some kind of strange adult-themed carnival. I also wanted to see Mumma's reaction to this, especially considering the fact that she was the one who insisted to see the Soi.

She didn't look impressed at all and had a disapproving look on her face. She stayed quiet, but I could tell from her movements that she was, actually, curious about all this. Her only concern was me—a young 12-year-old, who was not ready for such exposure. The only thing louder than her silent judgment was her impeccable ability to dodge the 'suggestive' pamphlets being handed out by enthusiastic street vendors.

Dad, meanwhile, was in full 'I'm so clueless' mode. He was trying his best to look oblivious to everything around him—like a first-time tourist who had just learned that the word 'Pattaya' didn't come with a free tutorial on local 'Soi' culture. He kept looking straight ahead, occasionally nodding, as if to say, 'Yes, yes, it's all fine, everything is perfectly fine', while subtly shifting his feet away from any 'questionable' and 'objectionable' establishment. But I knew he had complete idea of everything around. He wasn't fooling anyone.

We came out of that Soi on the beach side. I could tell from Mumma's face that the tension caused by the adult adventure had finally eased. Thank God, I won't have to feel bad anymore about being just 12 and accompanying my parents to a Soi in Pattaya.

Walking on the beach road, we stumbled into a sign that made Mumma cheerful again—Lakshmi Restaurant: South Indian Delicacies. It was almost dinner time, so we decided to have a look inside the diner.

The owner was standing by the counter. He welcomed us in perfect Hindi. It turned out he was from a village near Chennai, learned Hindi only after he came to Pattaya, and his restaurant was a hidden gem for vegetarians like us who needed a little bit of home. We sat down and ordered a full-on South Indian feast—dosas, vadas, rasam, sambhar, and a lot of other side dishes.

It didn't take long for Dad to forget all about the street chaos and focus entirely on the rasam-rice presented on a banana leaf. Or maybe, he remained nonchalant throughout. Who knows!

Mumma was still kind of judging everything outside; however, the food seemed to be working its magic. By the time we finished, she was less *serious* and more *I-guess-we-survived-Soi-adventure-for-now* mom.

And me? I was just glad I played my part well on the streets of Pattaya, without needing to ask too many questions and without letting my parents know that I was not that naïve not to understand the Pattaya night world—whatever.

Back at the hotel, we ran into Priaw again.

'How was the show?' She asked, a knowing smile playing on her lips.

'Marvellous,' Mumma replied, 'but just to be safe, let's keep the rest of the itinerary strictly PG.'

'What happened? Alcazar, I believe, is a perfect show for kids. I guess you witnessed something somewhere else,' Priaw laughed.

'Oh, the same thing everywhere. Alcazar was the only good place for families with young kids.' Mumma sort of complained.

'Don't worry, we have many things that are suitable for kids. Tomorrow, you are going to Koh Larn.'

'What's that?'

'The Coral Island. Not only Joy, but you too will enjoy there. There are many fun-filled activities.'

'Are you sure?'

Priaw smiled, promising that the rest of our trip would be perfectly family-friendly, with perhaps just a hint of Pattaya's signature sparkle. That is, only if someone doesn't get too enthusiastic and wander off into the flashy world of adult adventure.

We all laughed.

Lessons Learnt

1. In a low-cost airline, the in-flight entertainment consists of just a window, and your imagination.
2. An Indian abroad is like a GPS with one destination: 'Nearest Indian thali, please!'
3. A 'Soi' in Pattaya means a street where an accidental family outing may turn into a prolonged period of awkward silence.

Day 9

Pattaya

Any Indian, who has ever stayed in a hotel, will agree that the complimentary breakfast is the undisputed champion of all meals in a day. Actually, it's less of a meal and more of a survival tactic. Forget the five-star dinner or the fancy snacks; the 'real' event is the breakfast buffet. This is the moment when an Indian family goes from 'Let's sleep in' to 'We've got just fifteen minutes to eat like we're preparing for a marathon!'

My family is no different. For Dad, breakfast, while we are travelling, is a competitive sport, and losing means I'll get the 'You should have woken up earlier' lecture for the rest of the day. Here, I was enjoying the trip so far—and I was in no mood to spoil it by being on the receiving end—so, I got ready in a rush and joined Dad and Mumma for our first meal of the day.

The moment we entered the big restaurant, I noticed Mumma's eyes were scanning the room. I also noticed the relief wash over her face when she found that there were many Indian families sitting at every corner of the room. Until now, she had surely confirmed in her mind that Pattaya was meant only for single men from India! But now, she had proof that families could—in fact—travel here and live to tell the tale.

The breakfast buffet was—how do I put this—an absolute Indian affair. Only Indian dishes were served—parathas, pooris, bread pakoras, poha, and what not! Even a chaiwala was sitting in the corner offering masala chai in kulhads. After we strategically overstuffed ourselves, it was time to leave for our today's destination—The Koh Larn.

We hustled downstairs, grabbed our day bags, and piled into the cab. The driver was the silent-type, which was fine by us, considering the fact that we were not in a mood to talk yet. Furthermore, the jetty from where we had to take the ferry was hardly 3 to 4 minutes from the hotel. So, even if someone started a conversation, it was bound to remain unfinished.

At the jetty, a boat was waiting for us. As we entered it, we got to know that it was already bustling with tourists, and we were the last ones to get in. Our group attendant was a boyish chap. He bore an uncanny resemblance to one of my cousins—who happened to be an all-time class topper. This attendant guy seemed to be an interesting character, oscillating between being the life of the party and a strict headmaster. One moment he was cracking jokes and the next, he was sternly instructing kids not to take their hands out of the boat window.

After five to six minutes, our boat stopped at a mid-sea platform, which was looking more like a giant floating mall of adventure activities. It was packed with tourists, mostly Indians, of course—all enthusiastically ready to experience the kind of thrill you can only get when you're strapped to a parachute and hurled into the air by a speedboat. You know, the usual.

We climbed onto the platform and were immediately hit by the reality check that any adventure activity on a tourist hotspot mandatorily brings—long waits. The queue moved at a pace that could only be described as 'glacial'. It was evident that everyone had complimentary coupons and no one was ready to miss the thrill.

As we inched towards the platform's edge, I began observing the other platforms around us. There were two other parasailing operations—I had no idea which one I was going to end up with. They all looked the same—floating platforms with people wearing questionable life jackets and looking mildly terrified.

Finally, it was our turn. The staff handed us harnesses that looked sort of old. I wondered if they were even meant for safe parasailing! But we didn't have a choice, so we got strapped in. Then came a question from the man helping us with the parasailing gear—'Dip or no dip?'

My first thought was, *Dip*? *I thought I was here for a flying experience*! Still, I said 'dip'. Mumma was also in for a dip, but Dad seemed a little suspicious. Mumma gave him a nudge and said, 'Go for it. It will be fun.'

'Really? What will I miss if I don't touch the water?'

'Oh, come on! It will be an added experience. See, Joy is also ready for that.'

'Joy, when you're doing that, hold the parachute ropes very tightly.' Dad was passing instructions to me when Mumma was putting all her efforts in changing his mind from 'no dip' to 'dip'

'Yes, Dad,' I replied earnestly.

'Don't forget, huh.' Dad was persistent.

'I won't.'

Dad instructed me twice to hold the ropes, and I responded positively every time. But deep down we both knew that once airborne, I would definitely try to do a flying action with my arms. Thankfully, Dad didn't bother wasting his energy by repeating the same thing a third time.

After Dad changed his stance to 'dip', all of us were in the dippers club. A marking was drawn on our hands to confirm that we were not afraid of dipping. I was the first to go, tethered to a parachute, awaiting my *take-off*. The speedboat revved its engines and began pulling me very powerfully. Suddenly, I was hoisted into the air, and it felt like I was being yanked into an alternate dimension where time slowed down and my stomach tried to leave my body. At this point, I had no other option left but to adjust the whole unsettling posture by doing a full-fledged flying action by stretching my arms in the air.

I was high in the air, and from there, I saw Dad, desperately trying to say something to me. I couldn't hear anything as it was very windy around me. And I could not read his facial expressions from that height. I could not figure out what exactly he wanted to convey, so I decided to let it be and enjoy the stunning view.

And then came the 'dip' part. After a quick loop around, the boat slowed down and I was gently lowered towards the water. As I got closer, I realized that 'gently' might be a very optimistic term for what was happening. Gravity apparently is a thing, and in this case, it seemed to have a personal vendetta against me. My body slid downward with the kind of momentum you would expect when you're trying to get into a pool of pudding. Eventually, the boat sped up, yanking me out of the water like a ragdoll on a string.

And just like that, I was airborne once again. Water still clung to my face as I tried to adjust to the wind blowing through my hair. The boat completed its loop, and before I could really decide if I liked it or not, I was being lowered back to the platform—landing like a slightly damp pigeon in a high wind.

After me, it was Mumma and Dad's turn to brave the heights—trying their best to look casual while being towed through the air like a kite that had forgotten how to fly. As I saw them coming down, I was desperately wishing Dad to enjoy the thrill of parasailing so much that he would forget to scold me for not holding the ropes tightly. But, as my loving grandfather often says, if wishes were horses, fools would ride them.

After this exhilarating experience, our ferry started towards '*the*' Coral Island. As we approached Coral Island, our headmaster-type attendant decided to share a few fun facts about marine life—punctuated by random scolding aimed at overenthusiastic young Indians who dared to stand up during the ride.

'Did you know, the coral reef is home to thousands of identified species of plants and animals who were humans in their previous life? And you—yes, the stuntmen trying to stand up—save the adventure for the beach.'

We disembarked on the island, enjoyed some water sports, and had lunch which was organized by the tour operator. After rest for a while, we headed to Underwater World, eagerly anticipating a great diving adventure. Underwater World is a place where the wonderful world of the ocean meets the confusing labyrinth of safety protocols. The adventure began with a briefing session that could give strong competition to an ISRO pre-launch checklist. The chief instructor stood before us, doling out instructions with the fervour of a drill sergeant, ensuring every possible underwater scenario was covered.

'If you feel uncomfortable inside water, make V sign thrice with your fingers like this.' He demonstrated.

'Are we going to feel uncomfortable?' Mumma became a little anxious. She had the tendency of feeling uneasy underwater.

'Not necessarily, ma'am. But some people are afraid of deep waters.'

'Well, what if I belong to that unfortunate group?'

'Nothing will happen, ma'am, everything will be okay. We'll be watching you from here.'

'What if something happens?'

'You give us the sign, and someone from the staff will take you out.' The instructor was at his convincing best.

'When all is well, give a thumbs up sign.' He continued, and I found myself lost in a sea of instructions. Was I supposed to tap my helmet thrice if my oxygen mask fogged up? Or should I give a thumbs up when I see a particularly interesting sea creature?

'And remember guys, no talking underwater.' He added, as if we might forget that with an oxygen mask on our faces, we won't be able to utter even a single word, and still start a debate on whether RCB is going to win the IPL this year! Even if we did, I wasn't particularly sure that RCB guys would be hearing us and give their best in the tournament.

We, including Mumma, geared up—donning oxygen masks that felt like wearing an overly tight fancy-dress costume. Along with fifteen to twenty other tourists, we were herded into water one after another, looking like a school of awkward, floundering sea creatures. The staff members, armed with underwater cameras, were busy taking pictures of us.

As we descended into the underwater aquarium, the silence of the 'deep' enveloped us. All types of communication—including discussions on the chances of a particular team doing well in a cricket league—now relied entirely on hand signals. It was a surreal experience, floating among sea creatures and corals, with only the sound of our own breathing filling our ears. That's when I saw Mumma giving the 'uncomfortable' sign—with the enthusiasm of someone hailing a taxi in a hailstorm.

My immediate thought was, *Is she genuinely having a problem, or is she just curious to see if someone really comes to help her out*. Given Mumma's penchant for over-preparedness, it was equally likely that this was the only instruction she remembered from the briefing. Great! She must have been like, *You told me that the V-sign-three-times is what I need to come out of water—and here it is. Now it's your turn to act. Come and take me out from this place where I can't even give verbal directions to my family.*

The organizers were true to their word. As I watched Mumma, a diver swam over—concerned. Mumma waved him off, flashing a 'thumbs-up' sign now, adding to the confusion. The poor diver couldn't make sense of the situation. In fact, none of us could—confusion everywhere.

Dad, with an experience of over fifteen years of decoding such tricky situations, somehow understood what Mumma had in mind. He firmly gave a thumbs-up sign with both his hands, possibly to show the diver that all was well on both his and Mumma's side. The diver returned the 'thumbs-up', smiled, and swam back to the platform.

We continued our aquarium tour. I was appreciating the sights with one hand, and trying to remember which hand signal should be used if I spotted a shark. Meanwhile, the photographers were busy capturing every awkward encounter. I was fairly sure that if every misinterpreted gesture had been recorded, Mumma would be at the top of the leaderboard.

Eventually, after a wonderful and eventful experience underwater, we surfaced—removing our masks and coughing up the last remnants of seawater. Back on dry land, I decided to enquire Mumma about the confusion in the deeps.

'Ma, did you really feel uncomfortable?' I asked.

Mumma shrugged, 'I just wanted to see if they were paying attention.'

'You know, I thought that was the only instruction you could recall there.'

'They said it was important, right?'

'Yes, they did.'

'In fact, I remembered two—this one, and the "all is well" sign. And I made sure I used both.'

'Very smart.'

'Yes, very smart. How many signals did you use? None?'

'I didn't get a chance, Ma. Plus, I didn't get this great idea of managing to turn a potential emergency into a test of the system's efficiency.'

We had a good laugh, realizing the fact that in the midst of our adventure, even in the depths of the sea, Mumma's curiosity, Dad's ability to control the situation, my evident lack of creative ideas, and our collective sense of humour remained buoyant.

Priaw joined us in our back journey to the hotel. She looked relaxed upon seeing us in a cheerful mood.

'I thought I should say my goodbyes here, as you guys will be leaving for Bangkok tomorrow morning. I've arranged for a pick up at 9.30 a.m.'

'So sweet of you. You have taken good care of us. We were not this lucky in Singapore with our tour manager,' Dad said, appreciating Priaw's efforts.

'I'm sure there must have been some miscommunication,

sir. Generally, our Agency briefs the tour managers well. I apologize on their behalf.' Priaw was graceful.

'Oh no, you don't have to. In fact, the guys at the back end in your agency were always available, and they sorted out everything.'

Priaw then turned towards Mumma, smiling, 'Ma'am, I hope the day was good.'

'Yes, thank you so much, Priaw, it was one of the most enjoyable days so far,' Mumma smiled.

'I hope nothing objectionable was there,' Priaw said, tongue-in-cheek.

'What, Priaw, are you forcing me to complain about at least something?' Mumma burst into laughter.

'Oh no, ma'am, just tell me if there's anything we can improve upon.'

'Well then, if you insist, I must tell you. It's about the ferry attendant who was with us today.'

'What about him. He is a very funny chap, I believe.'

'Well, he was funny at times, he kept the trip interesting for sure; however, I feel he may have some room for improving his social skills. What say, Joy?' Mumma said, adding a pinch of humour to the conversation.

I couldn't help but chuckle. Surely, the trip to Coral Island was a memorable mix of natural beauty, underwater stories, and unintentional comedy, courtesy of our attendant who—like my cousin—may have topped his class, but certainly majored in eccentricity.

Lessons Learnt

1. If you have to choose between 'Dip' or 'No Dip', ask whether the 'Dip' is free. After all, it's never advisable for an Indian to miss a freebie.
2. Places without *special* services for grown-ups do exist in Pattaya.
3. Make sure to use all the emergency signals you remember, just to check whether the guys at the back end are paying attention.

Day 10

Pattaya to Bangkok

We reached Bangkok at noon. Actually, we entered the city well before that—but as it happens, the tour bus drops all the travellers directly at their destinations, and takes an awful lot of time. Unfortunately, our hotel was last on the route, and we were the last ones to be dropped.

Now, we had nearly six hours to settle into the hotel, have lunch, and explore the surroundings. In the evening, we had a river cruise scheduled in our itinerary.

The check-in time at the hotel was 2 o'clock, so we decided to eat something beforehand. We didn't have to struggle to find an Indian restaurant. In fact, in many parts of Bangkok, there seem to be more Indian restaurants than any other cuisine. It wasn't surprising—the city was teeming with middle-aged, solo Indian male tourists, loitering aimlessly through the streets. This city, I've been told, has traditionally been a magnet for Indian men—single or otherwise. Seeing the pot-bellied men with receding hairlines, I couldn't resist asking Dad if he had ever visited this place before. Dad was very sincere in his response.

'No bud, it's my first time. But I don't think we're going to have any problem here. I've done my homework well.'

'Of course, Dad.' Thankfully, Dad didn't realize that I was speaking tongue-in-cheek.

Indian and Pakistani families were also around, mostly crowding the souvenir shops. All in all, Indian food of every variety was available. We went to a South Indian restaurant and found that the food there was delicious. We asked the waiter if we could meet the owner to appreciate the authenticity. The owner, we discovered, was a Punjabi. Dad asked how he managed to serve such an excellent South Indian cuisine.

'Oh, we've the best South Indian chefs, ji,' the owner responded happily, almost beaming with pride. He then spoke incessantly about how he found each one of his chefs from the remotest parts of India. His story seemed endless—almost making us asleep.

After satiating our hunger with delicious masala dosas, we walked to our hotel, promptly approaching the check-in counter. After check-in, the receptionist gave us our key card and instructed a bell boy to take our luggage to our room. We followed him upstairs.

'Wow! The room looks so ordered and beautiful,' Mumma remarked as she entered.

'Yes, it is,' I replied, smiling. Mumma had always found organized stuff stylish—as anyone would!

'Speaking of beautiful, we've the Chao Phraya Princess Cruise scheduled in the evening. So, let's get some rest before the trip. Our pick up is supposed to be here at 5.30 p.m.,' Dad reminded us.

We unloaded our luggage, thanked the bell boy, and got ready to sleep. I woke up, and looked at my Pro Trek almost like it was a reflex action and found out that it was 5.15 p.m. already. The driver would arrive at 5.30 p.m., I remembered.

That meant we only had 15 minutes to get ready. In a hurry, I woke up Mumma and Dad, not forgetting to tell them the time.

Somehow, we miraculously managed to get ready within fifteen minutes and quickly made our way to the hotel lobby. There we saw several drivers with the names of their respective passengers written on placards. I kept thinking to myself that any time now, we might find a gentleman standing outside, holding a placard with our names on it.

When no such event occurred even after 30 minutes of waiting, I finally asked Mumma. 'Where is our driver?'

'Ask Dad, you were the ones who made a fuss about the time. I couldn't even get ready properly!' Mumma said while blaming us for the inevitable delay.

Out of curiosity and a sense of obligation, I looked at Dad to capture his reaction on Mumma's remark. But Dad was completely oblivious to his surroundings. Apparently, he wasn't listening to our conversation. He was talking to somebody on the phone. By now, I had enough experience to deduce from his ghastly expressions that the tour operator was getting grilled. After saying something seemingly effective in a grim voice, he disconnected the phone and started strolling around in the lobby in an antsy manner. At first, he went to the lobby's front gate and stared at the gatekeeper for a while, then shifted his gaze to the still-empty parking lot. Afterwards, he went to the reception and exchanged looks with every receptionist sitting there. It was evident that this didn't give him any satisfaction. Then, he shifted his gaze to the oversized tourist map of Bangkok city behind the concierge desk and, by the looks of it, conducted a thorough analysis of every nook and corner of the map. Next came the inspection of the lounge area, where hotel guests were sitting quietly.

When nothing proved to be of any help, Dad took out his phone, and called the tour operator again. This time his voice suggested higher level of decibels. However, amidst the bashing, Dad managed to extract some good news.

'THE DRIVER WILL BE HERE IN 10 TO 15 MINUTES.' Dad informed us, not realizing that his decibel level remained the same. So much so that every person in the lounge turned around to see where the thunderbolt had struck.

However, Dad's voice seemed to have a magnetic effect on some people, as we saw a family of three—presumably Indian—approaching us from amongst the people in the lounge area.

'Hello, sir! Do you have any news on our driver?' The man excitedly asked us, as if he had been waiting for this moment his entire life.

'Our driver?' Dad asked curiously, and fortunately at a lower decibel level this time.

'Yes, the one that was supposed to take us to the Chao Phraya Cruise. I think we're going on the same van as you guys,' the man said and smiled.

'Oh, okay, he should be here in 10 to 15 minutes. But again, that's the travel agency's claim,' Dad replied and smiled back.

'My name is Adnan Malik, and I'm from Pakistan,' the man introduced himself.

'Nice to meet you, Adnan' Dad replied.

Mr Malik and Dad chatted for a while—about the weather, their families, and their occupations. Slowly but steadily, the small talk faded, and the two gentlemen found common ground in sharing their frustration with their tour operator. For the first time in this trip, we had found someone who truly understood our emotions, and was running the same race as us. During the verbal decimation of the tour operators, the van finally arrived—almost an hour late. And if it actually was *the* van, I am not going to lie—its horn sounded like music to my ears.

And there he was in full glory—our pickup diver—clad in blue denims and a casual t-shirt. The caption on his t-shirt was catchy: 'Right may always be right, but Left is not always wrong.' Wow!

There was a confused smile on his face. He didn't seem even slightly sorry about the fact that he was one and a half hours late.

'You Indian and Pakistani family going to Chao Phraya?' he said in a very incomprehensible yet funny manner.

'Yes, we the Indian and Pakistani family. You the driver?' Mrs Malik said in a sarcastic and cold tone, taking a stand for all of us.

'Let's go!' said the confused driver.

'You were supposed to pick us up at 5.30 p.m.! Please explain your reason for coming one whole hour late.'

'Nay, I am come on time, madam,' the driver replied with unwavering confidence.

'No, you aren't! And now, because of you, we are going to miss the cruise.' Mrs Malik scolded him.

'You no worry, madam, we reach on time. It is 6.30, we reach by 7.' The driver reassured us, and took us to his van.

Both the families got seated in the van. For reasons beyond my comprehension, Mr Malik's daughter Alia took out her phone, opened Google Maps, and put in 'Chao Phraya Princess' in the location tab. It seemed quite unnecessary at the time, or was it? Only time would tell, I guess.

'By the way, what is your name?' I asked the driver, hoping to familiarize ourselves with him.

'I am driver,' the driver replied, as if he wasn't sure anymore whether driving was his profession or identity.

'Yes, sir, but you might be having a first name, probably.' Even I became doubtful if he really had a first name.

'Hello! People call me Amansak.'

I was still not sure whether we qualified as people to have the right to call him by his first name. Anyways, as he took us through roads and lanes of all shapes and sizes, a robotic voice came from the backseat, saying, 'Turn left in fifty metres.' It was from Alia's phone. We all heard it clearly, but the person who should have heard it, didn't. Soon enough, the fifty metres arrived, and then, were left behind. Our initial confidence waned as Amansak peered at street signs like they were ancient hieroglyphics, trying to figure out where he went wrong.

'Amansak, we were supposed to turn left about fifty metres ago. Are you really taking us to Chao Phraya?' Alia questioned him.

'He he he, sorry,' Amansak said, with a *caught red handed* sort of smile. Chaotically shifting the van by a full one hundred and eighty degrees, he came back and steered it in the correct direction—for once. Perhaps he understood that this was one of the instances where *left wasn't always wrong.*

The families sitting inside the van also understood something. Amansak must have started right on time when he came to pick us up, but his navigationally challenged heart must have led him to a scenic tour—or detour—of alleyways and dead-ends, thereby making him late.

For almost 15 minutes, Amansak drove without any word. We were not entirely sure whether he was on the right track. Dad kept glancing at Mumma's wristwatch every 2 to 3 minutes. His expressions of serene anticipation gradually morphed into mild panic as the minutes ticked by. Clearly, he wasn't satisfied with the performance of our pied piper behind the wheel.

As the family's self-appointed mascot of calculation and time management, Dad knew very well that we would be late for the cruise—even if Amansak somehow drove with the speed and accuracy of a homing missile. The only question that remained now was—by how much?

Just when it seemed like we might end up in Cambodia instead of our cruise, Amansak had a moment of clarity, or perhaps just sheer luck, and we arrived at the dock. Our joy was short-lived though—we were five minutes late, and our tickets had been transformed into fancy bookmarks.

'Now what, Amansak?' Dad asked, trying desperately to conceal his frustration.

'Now what, sir?' Amansak asked innocently.

'We are late and won't get entry to the cruise. What do you think we should do with these pieces of paper now?' Dad said, showing him the tickets.

'You keep them, sir. Without these you'll not get to enjoy the cruise.' Amansak was still very calm. Or maybe he was trying to look so.

'But how, man, how?'

'You no worry, sir. Cruise guys my friends. All of them. You just wait here.'

Then he rushed to the guys at the entry gate and said some words in Thai. The guard at the gate shook his head and signalled 'three' to his mates. Amansak smiled at them and victoriously walked back to the van.

'Done sir, you three go.' Amansak said as he pointed at us, beaming with pride.

'And you, sir, will be the first ones on the next ship. It will arrive in just five minutes!' Amansak said to Mr Malik.

Yeah sure, as if his five minutes could actually be five minutes, I thought to myself. But kudos to him, as he somehow actually managed to sweet-talk his way into getting us onto the cruise. Perhaps it was his bewildered charm—or maybe the ticketing staff just wanted to avoid further confusion.

Little did we know, there was another surprise waiting for us onboard.

'Good evening, people, please show us your tickets,' one of the staff members said.

'Here you go,' Dad said, giving him the tickets.

'Sorry, sir, these seats have been transferred to another family due to your late arrival.'

Oh no, not again, I thought to myself. To be honest, my brain was not ready to process another crisis—just after dealing with Amansak's pyrotechnics. Meanwhile, the ticket guy continued with a monotonous, almost pre-recorded apology.

'Extremely sorry, sir. There is nothing we can do now.'

'Really?' Dad said in a cold tone, which made the ticket checker have his life flash before his eyes.

'Uh... You can speak to the cruise manager if you like. I'll take you to him,' the ticket guy said with a newfound clarity. Dad's technique seemed to be working.

Then came an exquisitely dressed guy—the words CRUISE MANAGER literally written across his face. Dad took him aside, away from us. I couldn't exactly hear what they were saying, but Dad was smiling the entire time. The only thing that was constantly changing was the expression on the manager's face. It seemed that his initial reluctance melted away as Dad delved into his bag of tricks—anything from persuasive charm to outright wizardry.

I saw both of them coming towards us. It goes without saying that both of them were smiling. I got to know that not only were we upgraded to the best seats in the house, we were also offered complementary beverages. Dad: 1, Cruise Management: 0.

The cruise itself was nothing short of magical. It was like being transported to a floating slice of India, complete with tantalizing Indian food, melodious Bollywood songs, and more Hindi conversations than you could shake a masala stick at.

The cherry on top was Mumma's impromptu performance. Encouraged by the enthusiastic crowd, she belted out a song that had everyone cheering and clapping. For a moment, we were stars of our own Bollywood movie—cruising down the Chao Phraya River.

So, despite Amansak's epic detours and the initial seating snafu, our cruise turned into a delightful evening of unexpected perks and cultural camaraderie. And while Adnan and his family had to endure an extra hour of anticipation, we made sure to toast to them with our complementary beverages, hoping their cruise would be just as memorable—minus the Amansak detours, of course.

Lessons Learnt

1. Choose your Indian restaurant wisely, and do not think you're Anton Ego. You may end up with an endless conversation, which may, at times, double as a lullaby.
2. Most tourists are divided by languages and nationalities, yet united by their disdain for their tour operators' mischief.
3. Right may always be right, but left is not always wrong. Let that sink in, dear reader.
4. Use Google Maps, and you might just avoid falling prey to a confused driver auditioning for the next instalment of *Fast and Furious*.

Day 11

Bangkok

'Get up, guys. Its 4.30 already.' As usual, our morning alarm, who I fondly call Dad, was at work. I wanted to sleep some more as we had retired to bed at around half past twelve the previous night. But we had to be in the hotel lobby by 5.45, as the cab was to arrive at the hotel at 5.50. And I firmly believed that after yesterday's bashing, the operators couldn't afford to send the cab even a minute late.

Today we were heading to one of the most popular floating markets in Thailand, Damnoen Saduak—wonderful for photography, a culinary paradise for carnivores, a great place for picking up interesting items, and famous for offering a glimpse into a bygone way of life. Apparently, being vegetarians, we were not at all interested in the variety of food available there. Shopping? Yes, of course!

It was suggested by the tour operator to start early in the morning to avoid the heat and catch Damnoen Saduak at its liveliest. After getting ready, we came down to the lobby. It was hardly a surprise that the cab driver was waiting for us. And of course, it was a different one. This time, it was a smartly dressed young man who looked like he knew what he was doing. He escorted us to the cab with quiet efficiency.

It was a pleasant surprise to see that two girls and a boy were already seated in the cab. That meant, once we stepped in, the cab was at full capacity—no more stops, no more pickups, and we could head straight to our destination. In addition, the journey was not going to be boring. Damnoen Saduak Market was over an hour's drive from Bangkok, and all of us were visibly excited.

We introduced ourselves to our fellow passengers in the cab. The boy, it turned out, was Indian, while the girls were from Japan. The girls, Ishida and Kumiko, waved at us.

'Hi,' I spoke.

'First time in Bangkok?' Kumiko asked.

'Yes. You?'

'Not exactly. We are history students, so we keep visiting places which are historically important, such as Bangkok.'

'Well, what is so historical about Damnoen Saduak?'

'We'll show you when we reach there.'

I looked to my right to find the boy looking at me as if he was waiting for his turn. I felt like a celebrity. Seasoned tourists waiting in line to say 'hi' to a 12-year-old. Wow!

'Hi! I'm Mohit. I have a YouTube channel.'

'Hello,' I said, wondering whether he needed to add his YouTube credentials to his introduction.

'Nice, what kind of content do you make?' Dad asked, trying to sound more curious than he really was.

'Oh man, I'm a travel vlogger, and I've come here to make an episode on the floating market. I've travelled to a great deal of countries. You can watch my vlogs of Kenya, Tanzania, Uganda, etc.'

To be honest, he sounded like the kind of guy whose social media handle would be something like '@wanderwithmohit' or '@nomadicmohit'. Dad looked impressed by his obvious charisma, and so did Mumma, and he had every person in the cab subscribed to his channel within minutes, even our smartly dressed cab driver. They were starstruck, treating him as if he was the next Spielberg of travel vlogs.

Meanwhile, the history students took it upon themselves to educate me about our surroundings—which, apparently, were green, flooded fields.

'That's a traditional rice farm. Do you know the significance of rice cultivation in Thai culture?'

No, Ishida-chan, I do not. But you know what? I nodded, pretending I did. And, she took this pretentiousness as a sign of interest, and eagerly continued her seemingly endless monologue. This time about the rich historical significance of floating markets, replete with dates and cultural insights—while my brain, still in sleep mode, decided to take intermittent naps in between.

On the road to Damnoen Saduak, we passed through these charming little villages, where people were already up and about—engaged in their respective morning routines. There were little kids running around with giant baskets of fruit, old women washing clothes by the river, and farmers herding their water buffaloes. It felt as though the whole world had slipped into slow motion—a spectacular sight to behold, and a perfect picture of tranquillity, in my opinion.

A thought came to my mind, *Wait, why are these kids already up before me, when they don't have to visit a place so early in the morning*. Meanwhile, my soliloquy was shattered by an overly excited Mohit, who happened to be looking at the same village for completely different reasons.

'Bro… This is going to be a killer shot! Just imagine me walking through this village. I feel like I could make a whole series on this, "A Day in the Life of a Thai Villager." What do you think, Joy?'

I mean, the idea honestly had 'don't do it' written all over it, but his infectious enthusiasm made me believe that he could actually pull it off. And as it turned out, he decided to begin his 'bang-for-the-buck' project right there and then.

'Bro, is it okay to vlog people while they're working? Like, do I need their permission or something?' asked Mohit, as if he would actually wait for the villagers' consent before shoving a camera in their faces.

Our driver just shrugged in a nonchalant manner, possibly avoiding the question. But @wanderwithmohit wouldn't just leave without an affirmative answer.

'Bro, could you stop the van for a second? I can't let all these breathtaking shots slip away. Just for a minute, my man, please!' said Mohit, starting his third consecutive sentence with 'bro', while I sat there wondering what could possibly be so breathtaking about a random man walking in a village with a filter on. Or, maybe *bro* was trying to make a whole series on the secret lives of Thai water buffaloes! The cab driver, however, was smart enough not to engage Mohit's incessant flow of requests to take a shooting break. The cab slowed down only when we reached the floating market.

Upon arrival, we were unceremoniously ushered into a boat and pushed into the teeming canal. There were wooden houses on both sides of the canal. The boat driver slowed down to let us appreciate the winding waterways and catch a brief glimpse of those who lived along the river. Mohit 'bro' took this opportunity to film it all. His vlog was going to be a hit, I was sure—given the fact that it featured a hat-clad driver, a smiling Indian family, and two curious history scholars.

The journey took about 20 minutes, and it felt great to enjoy the peace before the hectic pace of the market. The market itself was a maze of wooden boats—loaded with colourful fruits, vegetables, souvenirs, and an interesting assortment of food items. People were haggling, shouting prices, and ensuring their boats didn't crash into each other. It was chaotic, but in the best possible way. Finally, we were there—stuck in a little boat, trying to navigate through it all. It was my first experience of a traffic jam on water, where hundreds of boats were trying to navigate the same narrow channels. Who knew Bangkok's floating market could rival its streets for gridlock!

It was interesting to observe my fellow travellers. Even though we were on the same boat—no pun intended—everyone had their own agenda. Ishida and Kumiko were busy giving impromptu history lessons, trying to address me, and mostly talking to themselves.

'This wooden elephant symbolizes strength and wisdom in Thai culture,' Kumiko said, her voice bright with excitement.

'And this lantern is used during Loy Krathong festival,' Ishida added, looking straight at me, as if both of them were being paid to act as guides to a clueless Indian kid. And me? I was barely able to absorb the priceless nuggets of information, having slept very little the night before. And let's face it—nonstop history facts can be a bit much for a tired twelve-year-old brain.

Still, I managed to nod politely, while secretly wondering if it was socially acceptable to nap in public.

Dad, meanwhile, busied himself playing cameraman for Mohit 'bro', who was now directing a mini documentary featuring bewildered shopkeepers. Bro was in his full flow, asking the vendors to subscribe his channel.

'Don't forget to click the bell icon for notifications.' He reminded them, as they stared blankly, probably wondering what an icon was.

'Mohit, try posing with this flower seller.' Dad pointed to a boat full of beautiful blooms. Obviously, he had greater aspirations than merely playing a cameraman. He was a full-fledged movie director now. And what was more interesting to see was that Mohit was gladly following Dad's instructions. And not only Mohit, the vendors were also being directed by Dad.

'You, sir, you smile for the camera. And don't forget to like and share!' Dad was completely enjoying himself. And why not? He was not just the director; he had just appointed himself as the marketing partner of Mohit's channel.

Mumma seemed oblivious to all this fun. As the boat was stuck in a jam and a souvenir shop was just there, she didn't waste the opportunity—and began her crusade with the seller. She wanted to buy a fortune cat with a raised paw, and had successfully managed to knock down the price when Dad temporarily abandoned his director's role to remind her of something.

'Isn't it the same cat you bought from Chinatown in Singapore?'

'Well, the size is different.'

'It brings luck, right?'

'Yes, it does.' Mumma was not keen to fall into Dad's trap of not buying anything from overpriced markets.

'So, having two cats means twice the luck?' Dad smiled.

Mumma was deciding an answer when Ishida intervened. I was quite sure Ishida was looking for a better audience than a sleepy, inattentive little boy.

'Hey, you know, dear—this cat has its origin in Japan,' she said to Mumma.

'Oh, I see.' Mumma was clearly more interested in getting the cat's prices reduced than to know about its origin story.

Ishida didn't take the hint and continued, 'This is *Maneki Neko*, a popular Japanese figurine believed to bring good luck and fortune to its owner. The cat's paw moves up and down in a swinging motion, and now they have started to make them with motorized arms so that they can wave all day long.'

'Yes, dear, I know. I've already purchased it a few days back,' Mumma said and started bargaining again.

Mumma's cold response made Ishida look for yet another better audience. Now she took it upon her to educate the shopkeeper.

'Do you know people keep *Maneki Neko* on the counter of their shops and restaurants, just to get more customers?'

And the bemused shopkeeper nodded, clearly learning about his bestselling product for the first time.

It became more interesting when I found out that Mohit was filming the whole thing. Of course, he was being helped with the camera angle, and so on, by Dad—who just got himself re-recruited as a vlog director. I wondered if Kumiko and Ishida had any interesting piece of historical information about YouTube.

The day unfolded much the same way. Mumma, despite innumerable impediments created by her fellow sailors, managed to bargain down prices—not just for *Maneki Neko*, but for several other items as well.

It's a different story that she ended up paying far more for each item than any seller in Bukit Bintang market would have charged. Or perhaps any other seller in any terrestrial market in the universe. But the thrill of buying things from a floating market was something else entirely. After all, it was not about prices—it was about memories!

Kumiko and Ishida kept on enlightening us with their impeccable knowledge of oriental history the whole day. Even when we left the boat and went to the food court, they continued telling us about the origin of food items ordered by us. Dad and Mohit—now a fully formed team—gave their best efforts to produce the lengthiest documentary yet on the floating market.

We finally concluded our trip to the floating market—with a bizarre yet entertaining blend of commerce, culture, curious historical facts, and comedy. We left with a deeper appreciation for the chaos of water traffic, a few more YouTube subscribers for Mohit bro, and a newfound respect for early risers, who somehow experience a different world from the rest of us.

We came back to the hotel, where we had to pack our bags for our next destination, Bali. The next day, our flight was at 1.15 p.m., so we had to reach the airport by 10–10.15 a.m.—if we didn't want to rely on the help of some miracle man. That meant, we had to rise early again on the next day. Yes, sure, if the kids living in the villages of Thailand could do it on a regular basis, I could do it at least for two days. But for that we had to sleep early.

Mumma and Dad too were feeling sleepy after a fun-filled but hectic day. I, somehow, managed to sneak some intermittent naps during the Japanese-sponsored history lessons, but Dad and Mumma genuinely needed rest now. Mumma had spent an entire day bargaining in the market, and Dad worked hard as a vlog director.

As I was trying to sleep, my mind started generating

strange ideas. May be Mohit bro would send his footages to Dad for final editing. I wondered if Dad would ask me to suggest a name for the documentary. If asked, I would suggest something like, 'Floating Market: The Japanese Perspective about Thai History.' No, that would be too long. Mohit bro might not be interested in that. If that happened, I would make my own vlog some day and name it 'Joy's Guide to Surviving Thailand with Enthusiastic YouTubers, Talkative Historians, Confused Cab Drivers, and Inspiring Early Risers.'

Lessons Learnt

1. If you have a YouTube channel, you automatically have a huge fan following. At least, you think you do.
2. It is okay to buy the same lucky cat from two or more different places. After all, it's about the memories.
3. History enthusiasts may go to any lengths when it comes to flaunting the spectrum of their 'very relevant' knowledge.

Day 12

Bangkok to Bali

For the second day in a row, I got up early. After getting ready and having breakfast, we drove to the Suvarnabhumi Airport. We reached there well within time, checked in, and dropped our luggage. After the security checks were done, we had more than two hours left for our flight to Denpasar. We decided to spend the time resting in the lounge. I even managed to take a short nap after Dad assured me that he will wake me up at 12.30 p.m.

I was still dreaming about something very important when I heard Dad's voice.

'Joy, get up. It's about time.'

'Yes, Dad,' I said and tried to see the time on my wristwatch. And I felt a shock. My favourite Casio Pro Trek was not on my wrist.

'Dad, my wristwatch is gone.' My voice quivered with panic.

'Oh! Are you sure you were wearing it?'

'Yes, Dad. I kept looking at it when we were coming to the airport.'

'Check in your handbag.'

I checked all handbags. Mine, Mumma's and Dad's. It was not there. I was pretty sure by now that I had lost it.

'Where can it go like that?' Dad looked confused.

'Wait. Joy, did you remove it during the security check?' Mumma chipped in.

'Yes, I think I did.'

'And you forgot to take it back from the tray. Then it must be there only, with the security guys.'

We all took our bags and ran towards the security counter. Mumma explained the situation to one senior-looking security person. He seemed to be clueless, as his shift started at 12 noon. He called up his other colleagues and enquired. But it was all in vain—no one seemed to know about it.

'Ma'am, if you can wait for 10 to 15 minutes, we'll check the restricted items store,' the senior guy said.

'I think we can wait for about 5 to 10 minutes. We have a flight to catch at 1.15 p.m., and boarding has been announced,' Mumma said.

'Then you can write your address in this paper. We'll try to find it and have it dispatched to your home.' The security person was trying his best to help us.

We stood there for 10 more minutes while half of the staff busied themselves to find my Pro Trek. With every passing minute, I grew more certain that I was never going to see it again. Finally, Mumma wrote down our home address, passed the paper to the senior-looking security person, and we headed towards the boarding gate.

For the whole duration of my flight, I was feeling terrible about my loss. Dad and Mumma tried to cheer me up, but it was difficult for me to forget about it. Why didn't I pay more attention at the security check? How could I forget to pick it back from the tray? I should've been more careful! I kept thinking until I heard the announcement that our flight was about to land at Denpasar airport.

Our welcome in Bali was smooth. The moment we stepped off the plane and entered the arrival area of Ngurah Rai International Airport, Denpasar, we were greeted by smiling faces everywhere.

For unknown reasons, everyone seemed to be unusually cheerful—the security staff, the cleaning staff, people at the immigration counter, and our fellow travellers. Apparently, none of them had forgotten to pick up their belongings from the tray at the security counter.

After completing the immigration formalities, we walked towards the baggage claim area when I noticed a group of Indian tourists carrying their luggage while chatting amongst themselves. Most of them appeared senior citizens, though they were dressed in colourful traditional *batiks*—bright hues of orange, pink, and yellow. Their enthusiasm and excitement were contagious as they spoke about their plans for their Bali vacation.

While Mumma and Dad were busy collecting the baggage, I decided that I'll go talk to some fellow Indians. It seemed that after the Mahesh Rai incident in Singapore, the stranger alert thing in my brain had been switched off permanently. I had spoken to almost every seemingly interesting person I met—why this moment should be any different? Besides, senior citizens are considered respectable figures in our society, so what could possibly go wrong? Even if something wrong happened, surely it won't be worse than losing my beloved Casio Pro Trek!

Most of these senior travellers were from Gujrat, and it seemed each one had a unique story and reason for travelling to Bali. It was fascinating to see how they embraced the Indonesian culture, trying the local food, and indulging in traditional Balinese activities.

As we stepped out of the airport, I could feel the warm tropical breeze ruffling through my hair—even though it was 7.15 in the evening. I saw taxis lined up, waiting to take tourists to their respective hotels.

The airport was a melting pot of cultures, and the energy was electric. Then we saw a gentleman holding a placard with our names. He took us to a SIM card stall, helped us buy local SIM cards, and then escorted us to the cab driver. It came as a surprise when the cab driver greeted us in Hindi.

'Namaste, sir! Namaste, ma'am! Namaste beta ji!'

Wow! This guy seemed very friendly. We greeted him in return. Mumma smiled and asked his name.

'Ma'am, my name is Budi.'

'Budi, you speak good Hindi.'

'Ma'am, I also sing Hindi songs.'

'Wow! Let's go to the hotel. And yes, Budi, please do sing us some Hindi songs on the way.'

'Sure, ma'am.'

We started for the hotel, which was in Ubud—a little far from Denpasar. Once we had cleared the usual traffic of Denpasar city, the roads were relatively empty. It was then that Budi started singing a song from an old Hindi movie. And wow—he sang beautifully. After he completed this song, Mumma asked him to sing a song in his native language. As he started singing this song, we were utterly awestruck. Budi was, without doubt, an exceedingly accomplished singer.

After enjoying Budi's very impressive singing, Mumma asked him whether he had learnt music.

'Yes ma'am, I have.'

'Then why don't you sing professionally?'

'I do, ma'am.'

'You are a professional singer?'

'Yes, ma'am.'

'And still, you drive a taxi?'

'Long story, ma'am. And an emotional one. Like Hindi movies.'

'Go on, Budi. We're all ears.'

'Well, where do I start? Let me tell you that I always had a natural gift for music and, along with my singing skills, I could play several instruments with ease. I started playing music at the pubs and restaurants from a young age and quickly became popular in my community. People loved my music, and I started dreaming of becoming a famous musician someday.'

'And you continued to sing at public places?'

'Yes, ma'am, as I grew older, I started getting chances to sing in bigger concerts. Over the years, I became one of the most famous singers in Bali.'

'Then?'

'Then came the downfall. Unfortunately, I got caught up in the lifestyle that came with being a famous musician. I started partying more often and spending all my money on alcohol and other stuff. Because of my late-night parties, my music suffered, and I stopped practicing as much as I used to. My performances became sloppy and unreliable, and as that happened, people lost interest in me and my craft.'

'Oh, it must have been a painful time.'

'It certainly was, ma'am. Despite the warnings from my friends and family, I continued to waste my talent. Even for big concerts, I would either turn up late or not show up at all. It made a huge dent in my professional reputation. Very soon, there was a sharp decline in the offers and contracts I was receiving. Ultimately, a day came when I didn't have any work. I was no longer the popular musician I once was, and even my closest friends stopped inviting me to their personal events.'

'And?'

'And I became a victim of depression. I lost all my money, all my reputation, all my goodwill, and above everything else—all my friends and well-wishers. It felt like there was nothing left for me in this world. It led me to more drinking. Then, one day, while I was staggering on a street in a heavily drunk condition, I saw an old woman trying to cross the road. Apparently, she was quite old and was having difficulty in walking. I offered her help. I was so drunk, as soon as I held her hand to help her cross the road, I lost control over myself and fell on the road. The old lady didn't seem surprised. She gave me a hand and said gently, "Son, you are still too young to be helped by oldies like me. I know you have a good heart, but that doesn't mean anything if your body is not supporting your good intentions. Don't waste your life drinking like this." It hit me so hard that I didn't realize I was doing an injustice to my talent. I could have accomplished so much more if only I had taken my life a little more seriously.'

'Wonderful. Then you decided to get back to yourself, didn't you?'

'Yes, ma'am. I stopped drinking altogether. It was tough, but the motivation won out. I began working harder on my music. Since I was rusty in the beginning, I had to find a job to support myself financially. That's when this taxi came to my rescue. The only catch is that even after reestablishing myself as a musician, I haven't stopped driving a taxi. This has given me support in my lean days—I'm never going to leave it now, when the days are better.'

'Budi, your story is inspiring,' Dad chipped in.

'Yes, sir, I realized that I've been given a second chance,

and I'm determined not to waste it. I'll keep working hard and one day, I dream to be one of the most famous singers globally.'

By the time Budi completed his story, we reached the hotel. As we came out of the car, and stepped on the impressive looking garden of the hotel, I got the shock of my life. Facing me was a big hoarding with Budi's picture on it. It said that Budi was performing there at the New Year's Eve countdown party. I couldn't conceal my excitement and shouted, 'Wow, Budi, is that you?'

'Yes, beta ji, that would be me. On Saturdays, I perform here. As a routine performer, I've been requested to perform at the New Year's Eve party too.'

'Can we come to see your performance?'

'Of course, for hotel guests, the entry is complementary. For others, there will be a ticket.'

'Mumma, do you realize, we just drove with the biggest music star of Bali.'

'I'm feeling honoured. Not just because he's a big music star, also because he is a role model for all of us.' Mumma seemed as excited as I was.

'Oh no, beta ji, I'm not a big star. But I definitely aspire to be one someday.'

'You will be, one day.'

'Yes, ma'am, now I should take your leave, I've to go back to Denpasar.'

'Bye, Budi.'

'Bye, ma'am! Bye, sir! Bye, beta! See you at the party.'

As we checked in, all of us were feeling both excited and inspired after meeting Budi. Today, there was no activity listed in our itinerary, so we decided to rest a little and visit the nearby areas in the evening.

The hotel staff seemed exceptionally efficient. Every guest was assigned a relationship manager—single point of contact for all queries and requirements. Ours was a young, smiling girl named Pandey Putu. She showed us around and then escorted us to our suite.

Mumma asked her if it would be okay to take a walk around the hotel in the evening.

'Yes, ma'am, generally it's safe; however, try avoiding areas which are not well-lit. Actually, our hotel is a little far from the town centre. It's already 8.30 p.m. People sleep early in these parts.'

'Oh! So, no market nearby?' Mumma's voice carried a hint of disappointment.

'Ma'am, there are one or two shopping stores—but yes, no market as such. You can tell us if you need anything.'

'For one, we'd be requiring vegetarian food for dinner.' Mumma had already figured it out that daily nutrition might be a challenge here.

'That can be arranged, ma'am. I'll get you khichdi, pizzas, and samosas for dinner. You can come to the restaurant in half an hour—your dinner will be ready,' Putu said, and immediately informed the restaurant.

'Thank you so much, Putu. What else can we do here during our free time?'

'Ma'am, as you may already be knowing, Ubud is known for its rice fields, traditional villages, and spiritual atmosphere. There are many things to do here. You may visit temples, take yoga classes, hike in the jungle, and explore the nearby villages.'

'Are there any temples around?'

'Here, almost every house has a temple. Even here, in the hotel, we've a temple. But it must be closed now. In the morning, we'll have a prayer.'

'Wow! I'll join.'

After everything was arranged in the room, Putu gave us her mobile number, requested us to have a little rest before our dinner, and left. We, instead of resting, took a tour of the hotel. It was spacious, with more than 140 rooms and a huge garden, where they were planning the New Year's Eve countdown party. The property was surrounded by dense forests, beautiful villages and the Wos River. The best part was that our room provided a commanding view of the Wos.

We went to the restaurant to have the 'vegetarian' dinner that was ordered for us. Although the menu was limited to three already mentioned dishes, which hardly tasted as they should have, they were still delicious. But this was an alarming situation. With this limited menu, we could not expect to feed ourselves for the next few days. Since the market was far, there was no question of finding an Indian restaurant that was nearby. It was decided that we'll buy some ready to eat material so that if we get bored from this limited menu, we don't starve. But where to find this material? Mumma decided to take Putu's assistance again and called her on her mobile. Luckily, Putu was nearby and she immediately came to us.

'Putu, we'll be needing some Indian ready-to-eat meal packets. Where can we get them in Bali?' Mumma asked.

'Ma'am, generally, Kuta has a lot of Indian shops. Then Denpasar is a big market, Indian things are available there. But nothing to worry, as I told you earlier, just give me a list of things you want, we'll arrange them tomorrow.'

'Can we find a Casio Pro Trek in Denpasar market, Putu?' It was Dad. He could not afford to see my long face since the morning incident.

'Dad, I don't want it now. Maybe when we go back to

Dehradun, you can buy me one.' I really didn't want to buy a new one now.

'Why, Joy? You will be needing a wristwatch.'

'Later, Dad.'

Putu looked at Mumma with a confused smile. 'Is everything alright, sir? Can I be of some help?'

'Oh, nothing, Joy here has just lost his wristwatch at the airport. Anyway, thank you, Putu. You're such a darling.' Mumma laughed.

'Oh, you're welcome, ma'am. Anything else I can do for you?'

'Putu, you told us in the evening that we can explore nearby villages. So, while in the village, can we visit someone's home?'

'Yes, ma'am, you can—and you should. There's no better way of understanding the Balinese culture and daily life.'

'Can you arrange a visit to a local's home?'

'Ma'am, you won't be needing our help for that. The locals here are very friendly. If they find out that you are interested in seeing their daily lives, they'll invite you themselves.'

'Really?'

'Yes, ma'am. In fact, a lot of film-makers come to Ubud for shooting their movies, and they keep interacting with the locals here. So, the villagers have a habit of welcoming the tourists. And since you're from India, people may themselves be interested in knowing about your culture,' Putu explained, smiling.

'Thank you so much for this information, Putu.'

Then, Mumma quickly made a list of all the Indian items she wanted to purchase, including packets of ready-to-eat rajma chawal and daal chawal, and handed it over to Putu. After that, we went back to our hotel room, excited about the next day's plans. In the evening, the New Year's Eve countdown party was scheduled, and during the first half, we were to visit a Balinese home.

I was quite sure, it was going to be fun, even without my lucky watch!

Lessons Learnt

1. One should ALWAYS double-check their belongings in the tray after the security check.
2. Talent is a gift and it should never be taken for granted.
3. Value your sources of support in your better days, just as much as in your lean ones—even if that source is just a taxi.
4. You can enjoy khichdi and samosas in a Balinese restaurant, as long as you don't expect them to taste Indian.

Day 13

Bali

We got up early in the morning. As per the schedule, we had the whole day at our disposal. Even otherwise, since the New Year's Eve countdown party was in the evening, and we didn't want to miss Budi's performance, we were not supposed to go anywhere far. So, we decided that we'll go to a nearby village and meet some locals. We got ready, and after breakfast, we stepped out of the hotel.

Ubud is beautiful—I must say. The lush green terraced rice fields, beautifully decorated village homes, and smiling faces everywhere. Mumma was the head of our three-member team, leading the charge on her quest for cultural enlightenment. And what caught her eyes? Temples! Everywhere we looked, there was a temple peeking out from behind a palm tree or nestled between the pretty houses. Mumma's curiosity was piqued—we all knew when she was curious, nothing could stop her.

Mumma marched right up to one of the temple-dotted houses and knocked gently on the door. It was opened by a pretty-faced woman with a smile as warm as the Balinese sun. Mumma very politely introduced us in a soft tone, 'Ma'am, I hope we are not disturbing you. We are tourists, staying at a nearby hotel. We were just taking a stroll through the village, and your house caught our attention, it's really beautiful.'

'Oh, thank you, please come in. Where are you from? India?' the houseowner responded in an equally soft tone, and took us to the living room of the house.

'Yes, we're from India.'

'First time in Bali?'

'Yes, practically our first day here. We arrived late last evening. Do all the houses here have such beautiful temples?'

'Yes, it's quite common for families to have a temple within the house compound. It serves to protect the family and the home. Even in hotels, you will find a temple—it is considered important to please and honour the gods so that the guests enjoy their stay.'

'Yes, in our hotel I saw a temple.'

'You want to see the temple in my house?'

'Yes, of course. But only if we are not interrupting your daily routine.' Mumma could not hide her excitement.

'Not at all. I'll show you the temple. But not before I offer you something to drink. Please give me 5 minutes.'

'It's very kind of you, ma'am.'

'It is my pleasure; you are my guests. And please call me Prithiwi,' the houseowner said and went inside to bring some refreshments. She came back with a tray with three coconuts. We started sipping on coconut water as she guided us towards the temple compound. There were two shrines there.

Mumma asked her what the two shrines were for.

'This one here is the Sakti Kemulan for worshipping the producing power of God. The other one is Pura Dalem. In fact, my husband knows more about it.'

'Sure, Prithiwi.'

'Alright, my husband will come back from the rice field at 12. Meanwhile, I'll show you around.'

'Are you sure we are not taking too much of your time?'

'Oh no, I'll be happy if you stay for lunch. My husband will be glad to meet you all. I'll also introduce you to my daughter. My husband will bring her back from school,' Prithiwi insisted.

We all wanted to spend some time with her and her family, so we accepted her proposal. She gave us tour of her entire house. After that we settled down on traditional woven mats in her living room, chatting about many things. Mumma asked Prithiwi, 'So, what's it like living here in a village? How do people generally spend their day?'

Prithiwi leaned back, crossing her arms, and with a playful grin, replied, 'Well, most of the homemakers here have almost the same routine. Our mornings start with the birds singing. You know, they're like the village alarm clock, except they never hit snooze. I, then, water my plants, feed the chickens, and offer my prayers at the temple. That's my favourite part—praying to the gods for good vibes and a good Wi-fi.'

Mumma chuckled, 'Good Wi-fi is crucial! But tell me more, Prithiwi.'

'Oh, you want to know about the glamorous life of a common Balinese woman?' Prithiwi winked. 'Well, after the chickens are fed, my husband goes to work in the paddy field, and my daughter goes to school, while I go to the market. You know, I'm an expert at haggling.'

'Sounds like homemakers everywhere have this wonderful quality,' Dad said, smiling. We all laughed.

Then, curiosity piqued, Mumma asked, 'And what about your daughter? What's her daily routine like?'

Prithiwi sighed deeply, dramatically placing a hand over her heart. 'Ah, my daughter! She's at that age where her biggest concern is whether her Instagram reels get more likes than her friends'. So, she spends most of her day perfecting her dance moves, filming her videos, and editing them. It's a full-time job—I'm telling you. I keep telling her, "Honey, I know Insta is your life—now come help me feed the ducks".'

We all burst into laughter. This lady was so gracious, yet so full of humour.

Now, it was Prithiwi's turn to ask questions. 'So, tell me,' she began, leaning forward eagerly, 'What about Indian movies? I've heard so much about them. Are they really all songs and dance, as everyone says here?'

Dad laughed, 'Oh no, not anymore. There was a time when most of the Bollywood movies were a potpourri of dances, love angles, fight sequences, and a lot of singing. But these days, Indian film-makers are moving towards more meaningful cinema. I've heard that a lot of film producers shoot their movies in Bali. Have you ever met any Indian producer?'

'No, I haven't. But a lot of film-makers from Hollywood come here. Wait till my husband comes back. He has many interesting stories about them. I also wanted to ask about Indian food. Is it really overloaded with spices?'

It was Mumma's turn to answer. 'We've all kinds—spicy, sweet, and savoury. You name it—we've a dish for it. Moreover, spicy food is an art. You build up a tolerance. I promise, once you have a good curry, you'll ask for more. If you have time, and you allow me to use your kitchen, I can prepare something for you and the family.'

'Oh yes, I'd love that.'

'But since we are vegetarians, I can only prepare something vegetarian.'

'That's no problem. My family will be so happy to have a

curry. Generally, I can barely handle chili, but am willing to try anything when I'm with the right people.'

There was a knock on the door. Prithiwi's husband and daughter were back, and she introduced us to them.

'Hi, my name is Vidura.' The husband introduced himself—he had a pleasant demeanour.

'And this is my daughter, Dewi.' Prithiwi introduced her daughter. The girl said hello, and almost ran away from the room.

'Don't think she's a shy girl. She's just gone to her room to be ready for lunch. In fact, she's a chatterbox,' Vidura said, almost laughing.

His laugh was interrupted by Prithiwi. She said,' Vidura, I've requested our guest from India to prepare some Indian dish for us.'

Vidura became very happy and said, 'Why not, that will be wonderful. Why don't we all go to the kitchen? We'll continue our chit-chat there.'

So, we all walked to the big kitchen area. Prithiwi asked Mumma to select something from the vegetable basket to prepare the Indian dish. Ma took out potatoes, onions, and tomatoes and with Dad's help, started working on a dish.

Dad, while peeling potatoes, asked, 'Vidura, before you came, we were discussing movies. Prithiwi told us that you have many interesting stories about Hollywood film-makers, who come here to shoot their movies.'

Vidura laughed heartily, and chuckled, 'You won't believe it. These bigshot producers come here, thinking they can capture the 'essence' of Bali in their films. One of them asked if he could rent my entire rice field for a 'soul-searching montage'. I told him, sure, if you help me plant the rice. You should have seen his face. Priceless!'

The laughter was infectious. We were already imagining some middle-aged, sunburned producer trying to figure out which end of the rice seedling to plant.

'Then there was this beautiful actress—I keep forgetting her name. She came to my farm, saw me working, and asked if she could help me harvest the rice. She wanted to 'connect with the land'. I said why not, be my guest. She started doing the hard work—within 10 minutes, she was more interested in connecting with the air-conditioned hotel room.'

As Vidura's stories grew more outrageous, I couldn't help but wonder about their veracity. But truth be told, the plausibility of these tales didn't matter. His excitement while speaking and animated gestures were entertaining enough.

While we were talking, their daughter, Dewi, came to the kitchen. Vidura welcomed her and said, 'Now, Dewi here wants to be an actress. And given her love for the camera, I'm quite sure, she will become one someday. I'm waiting for the day when she will be a famous actress, go to India for her shooting, and ask the local farmers that she wants to "connect to the land".'

We all laughed and Dewi made a face, saying, 'Stop it, Papa.'

'Oh, my beautiful daughter, I'm only wishing a bright future for you.' Vidura said in a cheerful tone.

This family was so simple, I felt. The incessant laughter made the environment so lively. Then Vidura spoke again, 'I forgot to tell you that I too have worked in a movie.'

'Oh, tell me the name, I want to see that,' Mumma said, clearly very excited.

'Hmm, I don't remember the name. the only thing I remember is that the director wanted to film a scene with me chanting some 'ancient Balinese wisdom'.

'So, you did that?'

'I just made up some nonsense on the spot. To this day, some movie out there has a scene with me saying, "May your rice always be fluffy, and your mosquitoes always be on vacation!"'

By now, our sides were hurting from laughter. This person was unbelievably full of life. Whether his stories were grounded in reality or spun from the vibrant threads of imagination, one thing was certain—his knack for storytelling was unparalleled.

Lunch was ready. We had an Indonesian-Indian mixed menu. Vegetarian nasi goreng, gado gado with tofu, and potato curry prepared by my parents. Our hosts appreciated that the curry didn't contain extra chili and still was delicious.

After lunch, it was time to say goodbye to our wonderful hosts. We left that cozy home with our bellies full, our hearts happy, and a newfound appreciation for the simple joys in life. I was really feeling a little lighter, a little merrier, and a lot more appreciative of the unexpected humour that life could bring because, in the end, it's not about the temples or the mixed-menu meals or even the chance encounters with Hollywood film-makers—it's all about the connections we make and the wisdom we collect along the way.

After resting in our room for a couple of hours, we came to the hotel lawns for the New Year party. It was a warm, tropical evening and the air was thick with the anticipation of the New Year's Eve countdown. The hotel was buzzing with activity, its beautiful courtyard lit up with string lights and music floating through the air. One of the attendants quickly reached and guided us to an elegantly set table in the open-air dining area. As far as I knew, we were the only vegetarian guests they were having—yet they had prepared a special dinner for us. The variety of dishes was impressive—spicy aloo-gobhi, paneer tikka, peas pulao, samosas, Malabar paranthas, colourful salads, boondi raita, and mixed daal. Wow! It felt like a small slice of home in the middle of Bali.

As the spotlight focused on the small stage set up in the centre of the courtyard, we all turned to watch. A Balinese troupe in colourful attire started their dance performance. It was amazing. Then, one after the other, groups from different parts of Indonesia performed, presenting their rich and diverse culture.

My attention was interrupted when a member of the hotel staff approached us and asked whether we would be comfortable if one more guest joined us at our table. A girl from Hong Kong was accompanying the staff member. She too was a vegetarian and wanted to sit with us. Mumma gladly offered her a seat at our table. She smiled and said, 'Thank you so much. My name is Tracy.'

'Welcome, Tracy. You're here for New Year celebrations?' Mumma asked.

'Actually, I'm here for work, travelling around to check out locations for TV ads.'

I was intrigued. 'Wow, that sounds fascinating. What sort of ads do you work on?'

Tracy leaned back on her chair, apparently more comfortable now that we were chatting. 'Mostly lifestyle and travel related ads. I work with an ad agency in Hong Kong, and we scout for scenic places that have a story behind them. Nusa Dua is one of our locations this year,' she said.

I nodded, impressed. 'That's amazing. It's interesting to see how the locations are portrayed in media. I love literature, so I'm always curious about the stories behind places.'

Her eyes lit up when I mentioned literature. 'Oh, you like books? Me too. Do you have a favourite genre?' Tracy asked.

'Well, I am drawn to all kinds of books, but I love to read mythology,' I replied.

We continued our conversation, sharing thoughts on our favourite authors and books, while Mumma and Dad seemed more interested in the stage performances.

Our conversation was interrupted by a loud announcement over the speakers.

'Please welcome, ladies and gentlemen, the super talented singer, Budi, our star performer for the evening.' The voice echoed across the courtyard, and I turned to look at Mumma, excited.

'Mumma, its Budi.'

'Yes, I was waiting for his performance.'

'Tracy, does your company make ads about life changing stories?' I leaned towards her.

'No, my company doesn't, but I would be interested, personally. What's it about?'

'You know, this singer here, Budi, is actually the taxi driver who drove us here from the airport yesterday. He's got such a beautiful voice.'

'A taxi driver and also a singer? Sounds incredible.'

'Yeah, he's been performing for years, but he's had a tough journey. He used to sing in small clubs, then rose to success and became one of the biggest stars of Bali. Then he lost it all, his fame becoming his greatest enemy.'

Tracy seemed interested. 'Then? How did he bounce back?'

'Long story. It will be better if he tells it himself. You may like to do a story on the ups and downs of his life.'

'Yes, I would love to.'

Meanwhile, Budi kept on singing beautifully. The crowd was cheering for him. Budi's voice was soaring through the night air. I could feel the energy building around us. People from all over the world had gathered for the New Year's party—but in that moment, it felt like Budi's songs were transcending boundaries, connecting us all.

Budi caught sight of us, and with a wide grin, he dedicated the next song to *the lovely family from India*. To my surprise, the first few notes of the song sounded familiar. And then Budi started singing 'Tum Hi Ho'. I looked over at Mumma and Dad, who were just as surprised as I was. Tracy seemed curious but a little lost, not understanding the lyrics, but clearly feeling the emotion in the song.

I felt a warm rush of pride as Budi belted out a few more lines. It was as though his dream was coming true right there in front of an international audience. I was so happy for him.

But it wasn't over yet—more surprises were waiting. After his performance, Budi thanked everyone and came straight to our table. Wow! Now, our table was the centre of attraction. Mumma introduced him to Tracy, and all of us started chatting.

As the night wore on, the countdown to midnight began. The whole courtyard was filled with excitement. People raised their glasses and joined in the cheer.

Then, Tracy announced, 'Budi, I'm impressed by your story. I want you to be an international star. Can I do a story on your success?'

Budi seemed surprised and confused at the same time. He looked at me—I winked. Dad smiled and told Budi, 'Tracy works for an ad agency, but she also makes films independently.'

Budi grinned. 'Thank you so much for supporting me.'

'So, can I contact you tomorrow? We may go to Nusa Dua together and discuss the plan.' Tracy smiled.

'Sure. Will madam need a taxi?'

All of us laughed. I was feeling so happy for Budi.

'Five…four…three…' the countdown echoed across the courtyard, and I glanced over at Mumma, Dad, Budi, and Tracy—all of them smiling and ready to usher in the New Year.

'Two…one! The crowd erupted into applause, laughter, and cheers. We all hugged, danced, and celebrated under the twinkling lights—the music pulsing through the warm Balinese air. It felt like the perfect way to ring in the New Year, surrounded by new friends, good food, and great memories.

Lessons Learnt

1. Wi-Fi is a crucial service in a rural Balinese household. In fact, anywhere in the world.
2. Mixed-menu meals are always the tastiest, especially when they are cooked by smiling people.
3. Enjoy the little things in life, for they often shape your outlook on the bigger ones.
4. The universe works in wonderful ways sometimes, say, by arranging a meeting between a singer and a film producer.

Day 14

Bali

Putu called us in the morning to inform that our cab had arrived, and we were expected to be ready in half an hour. This was not an issue anymore. For the past two weeks, we'd been following almost the same set of instructions, and we had already embraced this lifestyle. Get up, be ready in super quick time, grab your breakfast while checking the time in your mobile, and get going.

Today it was a bit different. It was the last day of our epic trip, and I was already dreading going home and facing my panicky friends. Tomorrow evening, we'll be on the flight back to India, and the routine will change. But hey, we still had some adventures left—I wanted to enjoy them completely.

According to the schedule, we were going to the Upside Down World in Denpasar, then to Tanah Lot temple, and finally to a beach nearby. We got ready and reached the cab, only to find that there was a totally different face on the driver's seat. Oh yes, Budi was with Tracy today, and possibly by now, they'd have found out some beautiful locations for Tracy's documentary or Budi's music video.

'Hello, Sir. I'm Usman,' the new driver introduced himself.

'Hello, Usman. You too sing Hindi songs?' Mumma asked jokingly.

'No, Ma'am, why?' Usman looked confused.

'Oh, nothing.'

'Ma'am, Sir, we'll first go to the Upside Down place.'

'Sure, Usman. What's special there?'

'Hmm, it's basically a house where everything is turned upside down. You take pictures there.' He tried to explain, but the explanation was not enough to draw a clear picture. I could only make out that it must be an interesting place, otherwise the tour operators wouldn't have added it to our itinerary.

It was only after we reached there, I found out it was an Instagrammer's dream, in the form of a nightmare of awkward angles and uncomfortable poses. While the place was designed to mess with your sense of gravity and perspective, what most people don't realize is that it's actually a great place to test your 'acting skills'. And when I say acting skills, I mean pretending you're not about to trip over a lamp or accidentally fall on your face while attempting a 'ceiling pose.'

Every corner we went to, there was a new opportunity to snap an absurd photo. I got pictures taken while trying to lie on the 'ceiling', posed as a Balinese farmer, acted as if I was getting a haircut from a very large-headed barber and a lot of other pictures that required me to pose in some really uncomfortable positions. Dad and Mumma were also enjoying the place, even though it was like taking a wrong turn into a weird house, designed by a toddler with a funny sense of direction and a broken GPS.

The place was good and enjoyable—but there was a problem. The staff members, despite having a smiling face all along, were not able to help much. Every room was a new upside-down exhibit, and whenever we had difficulties in finding out the next room, we asked them for directions. They just shrugged and smiled more, as if they were standing there just to keep an eye on us. After several failed attempts, we finally managed to get the attention of one member. She, somehow, agreed to guide us, but I could have sworn she was doing it out of sheer pity. Like, 'fine, I'll show you, but rest assured, I'll make you feel more lost anyway.'

But yes, at least we got some cool photos, which I was definitely going to show my friends, particularly, Kriti's brother Daksh. Given his expertise in creating 'scenes', this might be a perfect place for him, where he could pose in 3D 'scenes', without actually causing a problem for his folks.

We came out of the Upside Down world, and found our driver waiting for us. For sure, he knew that we won't be taking long inside this place. For no reason, I suddenly thought about Amansak, our driver who caused utter confusion while going to the Chao Phraya Cruise in Bangkok. Usman—and for that matter—all other drivers had been very sincere and efficient after that episode. The tour agency had definitely taken a notice of the inconvenience we had to go through.

While driving us to the next destination, the Tanah Lot temple, Usman smiled and asked, glancing at us through the rearview mirror like he was about to reveal some top-secret knowledge.

'Do you know about the Bali Breakup Curse?'

'And what would be that?' Dad seemed curious.

Now, I don't know about others, but when someone says 'curse', my brain goes straight into 'crazy tourist trap' mode. I mean, Bali is amazing, but there was no way I was falling for some 'love spell' gimmick, right?

Usman went on, 'Legends say that if a couple comes to

Bali and visits the Tanah Lot temple, they are cursed to break up.'

'Are you serious, Usman?' Dad looked surprised.

Of course, at this point, I couldn't help but smirk. My parents, completely oblivious, had totally tuned out of the conversation. It was like they were happily floating along, unaware that their relationship might have been one awkward temple visit away from a dramatic split.

'Yes, sir. But you don't have to worry as long as you are married. It's only for unmarried couples, and I firmly believe you two are officially married.' Usman laughed.

I could literally feel Dad and Mumma having a sigh of relief. Now that they were sure the temple visit would not hamper their fifteen-year-long relationship, they could finally listen to Usman's story with genuine interest. Usman, on the other hand was enjoying himself. He actually started telling us about how many couples he'd driven to this historic temple, who *did* end up breaking after the trip.

'It's like clockwork, sir. They think it's a romantic getaway, and despite my warnings, insisted on going there. And by the time they got home, it was all over.'

'Then why do the tour operators include it in the tour schedule?' Mumma asked.

'Ma'am, they do it only for married couples or single persons. These unmarried couples I'm talking about, just want to test the intensity of their love, I guess.'

'That's interesting.'

'Not for them, ma'am.' Usman chuckled.

'What's the story behind it?'

'Ma'am, I can only tell my version, which I've heard over the years. It may be true, it may not.'

'Alright, go on.'

'They say that many years ago, a Hindu prince and a Hindu princess came to Bali from Java. Their story went well until they decided to go to the Tanah Lot temple. They had heard about this temple's incredible sunset view. In the throes of this romantic vision, the two royals engaged in some hanky-panky.'

'Really?' Dad said. I guess he was praying in his mind that I don't understand the expression. I kept a straight face to support his thinking, the same way I did in Pattaya, when we mistakenly entered an adult street. After all I was just twelve.

Usman continued, 'Yes sir, and after this, as it happens in such situations, the prince left the princess in the early morning, then refused to have any relations with her.'

'Then?'

'The princess was ashamed of how easily she had become intimate and she uttered a curse on all future couples who visit Tanah Lot in an unwed state. She said their relationships would fail within six months after visiting this temple.'

'Is that what she said?'

'Well, there are several variations of the curse. As I said earlier, I've only heard from elders. I can't be sure what exactly she said, or if this really happened,' Usman answered sincerely.

Tanah Lot temple is gorgeous—great architecture, mind-blowing history, strong vibes of cultural richness, and a whole lot of monkeys. Seriously, it was like the monkeys had their own VIP section in the temple, cavorting around like they own the place. So much so that I was half expecting their leader to start handing out autographs.

We were told that the temple committee organizes a cultural dance show every day. Today, it was a show based on a *Mahabharata* story. Unfortunately for us, it was scheduled late in the evening, so we missed it.

We finally completed the trip to Tanah Lot without any noticeable relationship hiccups. I was definitely focused on ensuring Dad and Mumma were okay, so I kept asking them, 'Dad, Mumma, are you alright? Can you hear the curse of the ancient Javanese princess?'

Of course, I wasn't being serious. I mean, even if it was a curse, it wasn't going to affect Dad and Mumma, as they were officially, and properly, married.

'Get lost,' Dad said with a hearty laugh.

Mumma, on the other hand, looked at me like I was a walking disaster, but I could tell she too was having a laugh. At least until one of the generals of the monkey-army started trying to snatch her bag.

While coming back, Usman casually mentioned that the next stop was Padang Padang Beach. Oh! Yet another beach! I mean, don't get me wrong, the beaches in Bali are gorgeous; however, by this point, I was pretty sure I had seen a lot of sand in this trip. Plus, Mumma had other plans. And those plans involved something much, much more important than yet another postcard-worthy beach.

'Can we go somewhere else?' asked Mumma.

'You say, ma'am.'

'Like a local market.'

'Yes, we can. Denpasar has many such markets. What exactly do you want to take?'

'Well, nothing in particular. Just want to see a local market.'

Up to this point, I was pretty sure that Mumma wants to see the local market because of her sheer love for shopping. But even I was surprised, when she opened her cards.

'Usman, can we get batik-clad toys in the market?'

Oh, I understood now. It was all about finding Winky's partner. If so, then it was a mission with the highest degree of importance.

It all started five years ago when Dad went to Jakarta and brought me this small-sized teddy. It was dressed in a batik frock and I named it Winky. Well, that's the kind of sophisticated naming convention seven-year-olds come up with. Winky was cute, and I used to include her in my games a lot, but she had one minor issue. She was alone—and as any rational seven-year-old, who occasionally liked to make 'stuffed animal families' a priority, would tell you: no teddy should be without a family.

It was very difficult to find a partner for her in Dehradun. Even in Delhi, batik-shirted teddies were not very easy to find. I cribbed for some years, and then as I grew older, my interest in 'teddy matchmaking' affair faded away. Now, Winky was happily sitting in one of the tables with some of my other toys. She was more of a showpiece than a play-buddy. I had almost forgotten that she was still single.

Not that I was claiming to be too old for teddies—though I was mature enough to understand the real reason behind the Breakup Curse. But, as Mumma wisely pointed out, *You're never too old to find happiness in the small things*. So, as a responsible twelve-year-old, I nodded seriously and agreed. Clearly, the right thing to do was to find Winky a batik-clad family of tiny teddy bears—ones who could fit into her tiny batik life.

We wandered through the maze of stalls, feeling like teddy bear detectives—inspecting each one for size, cuteness, and, of course, the quality of their little batik outfits. It was like we were curating the most exclusive, adorable teddy collection on the planet. After what felt like a mini-marathon, we finally found the perfect ones—three little batik-clad teddies, ready to be part of Winky's new, super fashionable family. Mission accomplished!

I won't lie and say this didn't feel a bit childish, considering I'm twelve, and surely too old to be giving teddy bears 'families', right? But then again, I kind of agreed with Mumma: there's something sweet about getting happiness from the little things, and a cute batik teddy family is a pretty solid example of that.

Since we were in the market—with no shortage of Indian restaurants—it would have been criminal not to taste the Balinese version of Indian food. Otherwise, it was better not to bother our hotel chefs to experiment with Indian dishes. We took dinner in a restaurant owned by a Punjabi. Yes, no points for guessing.

While coming back to the hotel, Usman was once again in his talkative mode.

'Ma'am, did you take any souvenirs from the market?'

'Yes, we did. And these souvenirs are definitely going to be with us for a long time,' Mumma said in a tone that clearly reflected a very satisfied mindset.

'You have your flight back to India tomorrow evening. If you want, I can take you to Kuta in the morning. Kuta is very popular with Indians, you know!'

'Yes, sure. We'll be disowned by friends back home if we tell them we were in Bali and didn't visit Kuta even once.'

'Really?'

Dad and Mumma looked at each other and laughed. And I was feeling thankful to myself that I didn't bring Winky with us. Now her partner was with us, and if both were together here in Bali, and we somehow decided to take them to Tanah Lot, then that would have been a disaster, right? After all they were not yet married!

Lessons Learnt

1. If you're married and want to visit *the* Tanah Lot, keep your marriage certificate handy.
2. Doesn't matter whether you are a toy, a teddy, or an Indonesian—if your guardians are Indian, they will make sure you get a life partner.
3. Happiness doesn't always have to make sense.

Day 15

Bali to Delhi

The last day of our fortnight-long trip to South East Asia arrived like an uninvited interruption in a party full of fun. In just fourteen days, we managed to squeeze in more experiences than we could possibly have imagined within such a short timeframe. As the time of departure drew near, I felt a strange, deep wave of emotion creeping in. It wasn't because our trip had come to an end—a fourteen-day refreshing vacation was sufficient to gear me up for the struggles at school. It was mainly because of the farewell we received from the hotel staff—led by Putu.

Here, I should be thankful to Putu, who was our personal Bali concierge. It was because of her efforts that we managed to get Indian vegetarian food in a hotel in a village in Ubud. She took care of our comfort, arranged for our village excursion, and was always just one call away whenever we needed anything. While giving her a farewell hug, I felt like I was leaving a family member behind. And I knew for sure, Dad and Mumma too must have felt the same way.

Suddenly, Budi turned up out of nowhere. Casually strolling into the lobby, he appeared with a wide grin.

'Is that it, Sir?' he asked.

'Oh Budi! How have you been, man?' Dad was pleasantly surprised to see him.

'Putu called me and said you guys were leaving, so I thought I would drop by for a hug!'

'So nice of you to come, brother. Try scheduling one of your concerts in Dehradun,' Dad said and hugged him. After all, Budi wasn't just any driver—he was an inspiration to all of us. We had known him for only for a couple of days, and still, it felt like he was an honorary member of our squad.

I think I might have even shed a tear, but it's hard to tell—because I was laughing through it all, trying to hide the fact that I might just be a little too emotionally invested in this tropical vacation.

As we waved goodbye to Putu, Budi and the rest of the staff, it hit me: Bali, of all the places we visited on this trip, wasn't just a vacation. It was a place that somehow managed to make strangers feel like family. I'll always have the memory of how the people of Bali made me feel like the most important tourist on the island, even if just for three days. During the entire trip, we stayed in different hotels, in different countries. But checking out had never been this hard. I mean, they all were very professional, and they took care of us with utmost responsibility. Still, the personal touch provided by the people in Bali was missing everywhere else.

Usman announced that we'll go to Kuta Beach first, and from there, straight to the airport. As we approached near Kuta, we faced more and more congestion on the road. Apparently, Usman could not exactly assess the inflow of tourists into this area, given it was January 2nd, the next day after the New Year. Naturally, everyone, including us, who didn't get a chance to 'party on the beach' on New Year's Eve was now here to check out the aftermath. After all, who doesn't want to witness an area with more people than the total population of some countries? If you've ever wanted to experience the chaos of a city and think, 'Yes, this is what my vacation should feel like,' then Kuta's your place.

The beach? It was stunning! The traffic? Well—let's just say it was more of a tourist attraction than the sand and surf. In fact, tourists attracting more of their own kind!

At one point, we were stuck on the road for 20 minutes, and I thought, *Cool, at least I've got plenty of time to plan how I will tackle my 'particularly nervous' friend when I meet him after reaching Dehradun!*

Traffic is apparently the local hobby here. They should just hand out medals for 'Most Patient Tourist' because if I had any other emotion left besides confusion, it would've been frustration. But I guess that's what travel is about, right? From Singapore's squeaky-clean streets to Malaysia's skyscrapers, and from Thailand's chaotic tuk-tuks to this full-on Kuta Beach Karnival. It was an adventure. A real-life simulation of what happens when you mix travel, traffic, and too many people in one place. But hey—it makes for a good story, doesn't it?

Kuta is generally full of Indian tourists throughout the year, and it being the New Year time, there were Indian faces everywhere. Although I didn't know anyone, yet they all seemed familiar to me. Much like the enthusiastic senior citizens dressed in colourful batiks I met at the airport on my arrival here, telling me that they were here to embrace the Balinese culture. Here, however, they seemed far more interested in Indian culture. I saw them crowding the Gujarati restaurant where we chose to have our lunch.

After lunch, we headed straight to the airport. Our flight to Delhi was at 6.30 p.m., and we didn't want to risk being late. We reached early, and all the formalities were completed within no time. I had all the time in the world to check the item tray at the security check—twice, maybe even thrice—to ensure I hadn't left anything behind.

As the countdown to our departure ticked down, my mind started doing what the mind does best—overthink. It was the time when Mumma decided to strike up a conversation.

'Joy, a million dollars for your thoughts!'

'The usual, Mumma, nothing important.'

'Like?'

'I was thinking of the experiences we had in this trip. The funny incidences, the inconveniences, the interesting people, and things like that.'

'Yeah, a lot of shopping done by me, right?' Mumma laughed.

'Mumma, I've this strange thought that the people all over the world behave similarly when they face a particular situation.'

'Hmm.'

'The street vendors always try to lure the customers, the tour guides always try to sound more knowledgeable than they actually are, and the hotel staff always try to be as friendly as possible. Even the people on the streets are the same everywhere. Some of them want to know about you, and start a conversation themselves. Some are not so friendly, and leave you alone. I mean, this is so much like India. What do you think?'

'Well, I think the world is vast, yet everything in it is interconnected.'

'True, Mumma.'

'Joy, what do you think were the key takeaways from this trip?' Dad chipped in with his typical management jargon.

'I think I learnt how to get up early in the morning, so that I don't miss the cab,' I jokingly said.

'That was great.' Dad joined me in my laugh.

'On a more serious note, Dad, fifteen days is not the kind of time frame that makes you an expert in anything, especially when you change the country every fourth day.'

'Too damn right, son, too damn right. But the short trips definitely make you an enthusiastic amateur at a lot of new things. You just have to be open to all sorts of experiences. You not only learn new things from locals, you also gather the wisdom they share.'

Boarding was announced, and we successfully managed to get on the plane without losing any important item. Once inside, I kept thinking about Dad's words. *Have I learnt anything from the locals? Have I managed to imbibe the wisdom?* In the past fifteen days, I had journeyed through four countries. Not enough time to tell myself that I've seen the world, but definitely enough to feel like I've had an epiphany that could only come after a number of cultural exchanges. For sure, I had learned stuff and I was definitely going back with an expanded worldview.

The learnings and wisdom Dad was talking about, didn't come only from the side of locals. I also watched Dad's problem-solving skills very closely, and this started on our very first day in Singapore, when we faced problems one after another, and Dad solved them quickly. I was very sure, even the Chennai girls we met at the Night Safari in Singapore must have learnt from Dad's performance that day.

Then there was Mr Mahesh Rai who, despite facing a hell of a lot of problems in his daily life, managed to remain calm and cheerful enough to start a conversation with me. Having to handle his Tamil-speaking daughter after his wife's leave application being turned down, and the maid running away, and still keeping a smiling face was something people should learn from.

The flight took off and my fellow travellers got themselves busy in using the entertainment system. Mumma started watching a movie, while Dad started reading the Airline's magazine. I was tired of thinking, so I decided to talk to Dad about the trip.

'Dad, about the takeaway thing you mentioned, I want to know whether it applies only to the kids, or to grown-ups too?'

'You caught me there, Joy. Now you'll ask me if I learnt something new from the trip.'

'Exactly.'

'Well, there's always a scope for wisdom enhancement, regardless of your age and experience. I was impressed by a lot of things. For one, the family we met in Bali, they were under no obligation to treat us so warmly. But still they not only entertained us, they let us participate in their daily life too. I'm quite sure they have well understood the real meaning of humanity.'

'Yes, Dad, that was incredible. I mean, we just gatecrashed and they welcomed us with open hearts.'

'There were others as well: you remember the street vendor in Chinatown, Singapore?'

'Of course I do.'

'He was so practical, yet so philosophical. When he wanted to sell his items, he was a different man. After that he turned to preaching mode, and told us some very wise things.'

'Fall down seven times, stand up eight. That's what he said, right?'

'He was so right about life.'

'Dad, I think Budi has been practicing this philosophy in the recent few months.'

'Yes, I'm sure of that. We met so many inspiring people, both locals and tourists. Magne, our self-proclaimed guide at Batu Caves is an example. Can you think of someone else who inspired you by their action?'

'Dad, we met this wonderful French couple at Sentosa, Mr and Mrs Garnier. They made sure during the visit of S.E.A. Aquarium that the fellow tourists get their daily dose of entertainment. They even weaved a story that Mr Garnier somehow knows the sea creatures' language. Just to make us laugh.'

'Of course. By doing so, they were spreading positivity all over.'

'What about Manish uncle?'

'Ha ha!' Dad laughed.

'Yes, Dad, ha ha!' I winked.

'Joy, Manish is a good man. It may seem that he's a bit more ostentatious than others, but he has a clean heart. Moreover, he has worked very hard for his success. In a way, he too is an inspiration for us.'

'Agreed, Dad. But let's be honest, I could feel a hint of sarcasm in the way you were talking to him.'

'Maybe yes, I got carried away by the way he was showcasing his success. Besides, I made him feel good during the conversation.'

'Anyway, he definitely has an interesting personality.'

'For sure, he does.'

'Talking of interesting people we met, what's your take on our driver on the way to the river cruise in Bangkok?'

'Oh, Amansak. He may have been a little confused—but in the end, he got us an entry to the cruise at the last moment.'

'Yes, he did. But he was so late that the cruise guys transferred our seats to someone else. If you hadn't applied your outright wizardry, things might not have been in our favour.' I chuckled.

'Oh Joy, you have to do such things to smoothen the creases, nothing much.'

Dinner was served to us. I looked at my food tray, and was happy to see a cheese sandwich. Wait, what would have happened to the sandwich I ordered at Sentosa Island? Maybe it was served to some other customer, maybe someone from the staff had it, or maybe, they never prepared it at all! Whatever might have been the case, one thing was sure. The sandwich story was going to give me a lot of leverage when I narrated my travel tale to my friends at school.

By the time our flight landed in Delhi, I had a brief but profound realization. At the age of twelve, I may not have understood everything about life, but I had learned something deeper than I could have imagined. I know what people may think. Fifteen days? Is that even enough time to form a coherent thought? But here's the thing—when you're constantly exposed to new cultures, new people, and new ways of thinking, something clicks. It's like your brain is suddenly forced to look beyond the small circle you've been drawing in your everyday life.

I mean, exposure to different ways of life makes you realize that there's more to it than the next WhatsApp notification—or which side of the bed you sleep on. It's about realizing there are people who survive without running water in their villages, who get up with the rising sun to make their ends meet, and are so polite that they'll apologize for existing in your personal space.

In these fifteen days, I had wandered through lands where people lived differently, yet somehow, we all seemed to seek the same thing—connection, joy, and meaning. It was as if every step I took, from the streets of Bukit Bintang to the waterways of Thailand, skyscrapers in Singapore to the green fields of Bali, had guided me closer to a quiet truth: **the world is vast, yet everything in it is interconnected.**

Oriental Wisdom

We reached Delhi at 12.30 a.m. IST. The plan was to stay overnight in Delhi and travel back to Dehradun by road in the morning after breakfast. With all the memories of fortnight-long oriental experience, we checked in the same hotel in Aerocity where we halted while starting the trip.

Despite having a mind full of mixed feelings, after fifteen days of running around airports—and trying not to get lost in foreign countries—I was more than ready to collapse into a comfortable hotel bed. My tiredness got the better of me, and I fell into a deep slumber in no time.

I got up a little late in the morning, as there was no hurry to catch up with the schedule for the day. Around 9.30 a.m., we went to the restaurant for breakfast. The restaurant was buzzing as usual, and I couldn't help but smile at the comforting familiarity of it all. It felt as though I had come full circle—as if the universe had decided to place me back in the same comfy hotel as a reminder that I had survived the chaos of four countries. Most of the guests had already finished their breakfast. The hall was full of Indian faces, and I genuinely felt happy to be back in India.

At a nearby table, I spotted a family deep in discussion over some colourful brochures. A man, a woman, and a girl about my age. It looked like they were giving final touches to their vacation planning. And probably they were going abroad, otherwise they wouldn't stay in Aerocity, I guessed. The girl looked at me and smiled. I waved at her. She said something to the woman, and came to our table.

'Hi! My name is Tejasvini.'

'I'm Joy. You guys going on a vacation?'

'Yeah, how did you know?'

'Oh, easy to guess. Brochures and all. Where are you going?'

'Cambodia.'

'Your first trip abroad?'

'Hmm.'

'Wow! We are just coming back from Indonesia. Before that we went to Singapore, Malaysia, and Thailand.'

'Oh, so many countries!'

'Hmm.' I smiled.

'You enjoyed it there?'

'Well, depends on your idea of enjoyment. If enjoyment is strictly following the daily schedule, then yes, I did.' I laughed.

'Was it your first trip abroad?'

'Well, when I was very young, I was taken to some countries, but I don't remember much of it now.'

I replied with a strange feeling of Déjà vu. Yes, this has happened before! The same conversation happened with Aryan when I was about to embark on the trip, and he only recently returned from one. The only difference was that the roles had reversed now. I was on the *wiser* side of the table. I could now relate to what Tejasvini must have been feeling. She was nervous ahead of her first trip abroad and wanted to ensure it would be enjoyable.

'Travelling to four countries in a go means a lot of good and bad experiences. Isn't it so?'

'Yes, I had both good and bad experiences. In a way

both are good. Good experiences turn into good memories, which you cherish for years. Bad experiences are not that bad though. They turn into wonderful stories. In fact, travelling is one thing that makes you learn enormously, if you see things with the right perspective.' I was definitely repeating Aryan bhai's words.

'We are going there just for six days. Is that enough time to learn something?'

'You'll have a lot of opportunities to talk to locals, fellow travellers, guides, street vendors, and the hotel staff. Don't miss the opportunity—you'll learn a lot.'

'Did you learn anything interesting?'

'Well, the world is very big, and there are lots of different ways people live and think. But one thing I learned for sure that there's no one right way to live. People are all same and different at the same time—that's okay.'

Tejasvini stared at me for a moment, absorbing my every word. Maybe she was thinking that I was sounding a bit more philosophical for my age. Meanwhile, her parents had finished their breakfast, and she had to go now.

'Thanks Joy. I'll try my best to enjoy and learn. Bye,' Tejasvini said.

'Bye. All the best for your journey.'

Both Mumma and Dad, who were listening to my conversation with Tejasvini patiently, gave me a look that was a combination of affection and appreciation. I smiled back at them.

We checked out of the hotel, got into the car, and started our journey back home to Dehradun. The views from the window were great. Even though everything was same as they were before—the greenery, the chaotic traffic of Indian roads, the street vendors, and the common people—to my eyes, everything seemed to have a new meaning. I remembered Aryan Bhai, who had spoken about life in the same way a tree speaks to the earth—calmly, without rushing, with a wisdom that comes from time and experience. His words about the journey of life had made sense to me then, but now, standing here, I felt as though I had *become* that journey. It was no longer about the destinations I reached or the people I had spoken to: it was the quiet unfolding of a deeper understanding, a kind of Oriental wisdom within me.

And perhaps that was the true gift I had received. Not in the form of experiences I had, but in the stillness that settled within my heart—like the calm that follows a storm. There is wisdom in every moment, in every person, in every experience. And as I sat there, I realized that wisdom, Oriental or otherwise, is not something you find by searching the world—it is something you awaken to within yourself.

Acknowledgements

Howsoever small or seemingly insignificant, the making of a book involves many long and arduous tasks. Writing this one has been a transformative journey, made possible only through the support, encouragement, and inspiration of many individuals. It gives me immense pleasure to express my gratitude to all those who have so lovingly showered me with their blessings, help, and guidance.

First and foremost, I wish to thank my wonderful family for their constant love and encouragement—my Baba, the late Dr Suresh Chandra Srivastava; Amma, Mrs Dayawati Srivastava; Mumma, Dr Rama Srivastava (Ritu); Nana, Mr Girish Chandra Srivastava; Nani, Mrs. Gagan Srivastava; my dearest Chacha, Dr Aseem Srivastava; and Dad, Dr Anand Srivastava. From reading early drafts and suggesting cover ideas to sharing creative inputs and thoughtful feedback, my family has been as vital to this book as I have. Thank you so much, everyone.

I extend my heartfelt thanks to my teachers at St Joseph's Academy, Dehradun—Mrs Tripti Sharma, Mrs Anuradha Tandon, Mrs Sonia Bhatt, and Mrs Anjali Bisht—for their unfailing goodwill, guidance, and encouragement.

My sincere thanks also to Rupa Publications, especially Mr Dibakar Ghosh and Ms Shatarupa Dhar, for their faith in this manuscript and their professional support throughout the publishing process.

A special word of appreciation goes to Mr Pradeep Dadar, whose encouragement, constructive suggestions, and belief in the vision of this book motivated me at every step.

Lastly, I am deeply grateful to all my readers and fellow learners whose curiosity and love for knowledge continue to inspire writers like me to create with purpose.

This book is as much yours as it is mine.